'Charlotte Wood is one of our finest and most chameleonic writers
. . . Wood's novels are often uncomfortable explorations of Australian
life: profound in their emotional scope . . . superb storytelling.'

Rebecca Starford, *The Australian*

'Wood is an agonisingly gifted writer.'

Marian Keyes

'Ms Wood's writing is direct and spare, yet capable of bursting with
unexpected beauty.'

The Economist

'Wood joins the ranks of writers such as Nora Ephron, Penelope
Lively and Elizabeth Strout.'

The Guardian UK

'Wood's writing reminds me of Helen Garner's, in that it's easy to
read, but deceptively so: it's rich with ideas and absolutely distinctive
in its voice.'

Jo Case, *Readings Monthly*

'Wood's writing crackles with vivid precision'

John Powers, NPR

'Wood makes the most ordinary moments glow: her sensitivity to visual detail cuts to the quick. Little escapes her, and the result is a graceful and empathetic portrayal of one family seeking to understand itself.'

Australian Book Review

'Charlotte Wood's writing is haunting, building tension so subtly the action hits like an unexpected blow. Her characters are wounded and human, their dialogue profound without meaning to be.'

Good Reading

'Sensitivity and acuity are Wood's strengths . . . remarkable in her forensic abilities . . . a captivating, questing writer whose work is well worth watching.'

Weekend Australian

'One of the most intelligent and compassionate novelists in Australia.'

Angela Meyer, *The Age*

'Wood's writing is made of the same stuff as Debussy's music: exquisite and sometimes dissonant chords; delicate, slow notes; a gentle, passionate witness of the patterns submerged within the real order of things; of longing and elegy. And of love.'

The Bulletin

'Such limpid and beautiful prose that Charlotte Wood herself should be celebrated.'

Sunday Age

'Wood is a consummate observer of the human condition. She distils the dynamics of families and the interactions of daily life, and writes about them with honesty and restraint.'

Australian Book Review

'It makes us weep in a way only the best writing can. It seems little accident that the book takes its title from a song, for the almost exquisite pain that Wood captures usually belongs to the realm of music.'

Sydney Morning Herald

'One rereads the novel not for its shock value but for its nuances, its deep questions and its lovely supple prose . . . vibrant, intelligent, utterly compelling work, achingly real and seductively woven with a restrained consonance of connected images that build through the novel to a final symbolic release.'

Adelaide Advertiser

'Wood has the ability to evoke matters of life and death without straining for effect. Her prose is convincing and her images precise.'

Sydney Morning Herald

'Wood's style is all intelligent observation. She maintains a sympathy for her characters even when their world seems grubby and hopeless. She weaves startling, specific descriptions into a plot without ever stalling or sounding pretentious. I found her descriptions of older people and upset children particularly moving, capturing humanity at its best and worst. Wood's books are an intimately rendered portrait of contemporary Australia and, as such, prompt readers to think about some of this country's real issues.'

Sunday Tasmanian

ALSO BY CHARLOTTE WOOD

FICTION

Pieces of a Girl (1999)

The Submerged Cathedral (2004)

The Children (2007)

Animal People (2011)

The Natural Way of Things (2015)

The Weekend (2019)

NON-FICTION

Love & Hunger (2012)

The Writer's Room (2016)

The Luminous Solution

Charlotte Wood

ALLEN&UNWIN
SYDNEY · MELBOURNE · AUCKLAND · LONDON

First published in 2021

Allen & Unwin
83 Alexander Street
Crows Nest NSW 2065
Australia
Phone: (61 2) 8425 0100
Email: info@allenandunwin.com
Web: www.allenandunwin.com

 A catalogue record for this
book is available from the
National Library of Australia

ISBN 978 1 76087 923 5

Internal design by Sandy Cull, gogoGingko
Set in 12.6/20 pt Garamond Premier Pro by Bookhouse, Sydney
Printed and bound in Australia by Griffin Press, part of Ovato

10 9 8 7 6 5 4 3 2 1

 The paper in this book is FSC® certified.
FSC® promotes environmentally responsible,
socially beneficial and economically viable
management of the world's forests.

In memory of Georgia Blain

CONTENTS

Preface xv

1 FERTILE GROUND

Nourishing the inner life 1

2 THE GETTING OF WISDOM

Finding your own teachers 12

3 THE GRUMPY STRUGGLE, DESPAIR AND
THE LUMINOUS SOLUTION

Nine kinds of creative thinking 19

4 UNCONSCIOUS BIAS

The dreaming mind 44

5   TAKE AN OBJECT

How art can transfigure hatred   55

6   STRANGE BEDFELLOWS

The Lady, the unicorn and
The Natural Way of Things   63

7   LETTING IN THE LIGHT

Sharing unfinished work: risks and joys   79

8   CAT AND BABY

On intuition vs pragmatism   98

9   AN ELEMENT OF LIGHTNESS

Laughter as a creative force   105

10   THE PAINT ITSELF

The world inside a sentence   122

11   READING ISN'T SHOPPING

Why creativity needs disturbance   132

12   THE OUTSIDE VOICE

In praise of unruly artists   152

———

13   AFRAID OF THE DARK
Anger as creative fuel 161

14   ON GODS AND GHOSTS
Catholicism, contradiction and creativity 175

15   *BETWEEN A WOLF AND A DOG*
Georgia Blain's final work 188

16   USEFUL, PLEASURABLE, STRANGE
Growing old as an art form 195

17   THE RAPTURE
Nature and the artist 208

Author's note 221

References 223

Acknowledgements 237

———

PREFACE

Other people's creative lives have always fascinated me. My writing room at home contains several shelves of books on the nature of art and creativity, collections of interviews with writers and artists, how-to-write instruction manuals, discussions of the elements of fiction.

These books happen to be shelved directly behind my chair: they have my back. There's something both cheering and challenging about their spines, many tattered with age or bleached by sunlight, the pages inside sometimes speckled with cockroach shit or the lacework of silverfish. In general, I'm not sentimental about keeping books—I don't have room, and I prefer to see the books I read as passing through my life like a river of knowledge and feeling. Occasionally I'll step into the river and pull one out to keep before it is swept past, but I eventually let the current take most of them. And yet I have never knowingly discarded one of the books on these shelves. I'm superstitious about them. I value their expertise and solidarity too much to let them go, despite not having looked at most of them now for decades. The feeling remains that they are indispensable companions and guides to a life that is often confusing, sometimes lonely, occasionally frightening.

The following book is a synthesis of everything I've learned about my own creative impulse since I first began trying to write fiction more than 30 years ago. I'd like to think of it as a conversation not just with those guides on my shelves, but with all the writers and artists I've met, and many I haven't, over those three decades.

I've been invited to publish a collection like this before now, but something in me always resisted. There wasn't time, I wasn't experienced enough, I couldn't see enough of a connecting thread and didn't want to make a random anthology of bits and pieces.

But in 2020, during the first year of the COVID-19 pandemic, everything changed. Life was suddenly both more spacious and more precious. We were talking about what we really valued, paying more attention to our interior worlds and the people close to us, suddenly aware of how little control we really have over our lives. In the early months of the pandemic I published a piece called 'Fertile Ground', about the disarray and panic I'd been feeling in my own spirit, and how I hoped to recover my equilibrium, both creatively and personally. So many people contacted me after reading it, to say it had echoed their own experience, that I began to think the time might be right for a book like this. A new version of that original piece now forms the first chapter.

Most of the material in this book started life separately, delivered as speeches or published in newspapers, journals and magazines at different times. But when I brought the pieces together, I quite often found I had more to say on a subject, or that I'd changed my mind and some earlier ideas no longer felt true. There was a lot of weeding to be done—of old sentences that no longer resonated, or even entire pieces that didn't now seem to belong in this garden I'm calling 'the inner life'. Some chapters retain only a paragraph or two of their original form, and several have never been published at all before.

Many chapters make reference to my 2015 novel *The Natural Way of Things*. I was asked to speak and write a great deal about that novel—about its formation and its ripple effects for me and other people—and it seems clear now that it also took a lot of processing for me personally once it was out in the world. But it was also the novel that perhaps taught me the most about my own creativity—about trusting one's instincts, about risk, about the potency of symbol and dream and archetype, about the exhilaration of departing from safe and familiar territory, of overturning expectations and understanding that there's always more to discover lying beneath what you think you know. Most of the mentions of that novel are about the lessons

I learned not just from writing it, but from the other artists and writers who unwittingly formed a vast, delicate yet strong safety net around me as I worked on it. I hope my thoughts about it might now contribute a thread of a similar net for other people straying into their own new creative ground.

While I hope this book might be part of a conversation with other people making art, it's important for me to say that it is by no means addressed only to artists or writers. As I say in 'Fertile Ground', a rich inner life is not just the preserve of the arts. The joys, fears and profound self-discoveries of creativity—through making or building anything that wasn't there before, any imaginative exploration or attempt to invent—I believe to be the birthright of every person on this earth.

If you live your life with curiosity and intention—or would like to—this book is for you.

1

Fertile Ground

•————•

Nourishing the inner life

The garden is in disrepair. In fact, it seems to me, peering through the glass kitchen doors this Saturday morning, that our pocket courtyard garden has never been in such urgent need of restoration. The sight of it fills me with an overwhelming gloom. Plants burdened with woody overgrowth sag into displeasing shapes, oppressing the more fragile, undernourished plants beneath. The leaves of others are shrivelled with disease and the birdbath holds only a puddle of sludge. Junk clutters the pavers: tangles of hose, the wheelie bin with its lid flung back, a pair of running shoes left out, soles up, for the sunshine to disinfect.

I have a powerful feeling that this disarray isn't just cosmetic but is symptomatic of some deeper malaise. The sense of spacious, considered serenity—surely the reason to have a garden in the first place—has died, along with half the plants. There's no order, no cohesion, no beauty.

It's the third weekend of our first lockdown of the coronavirus pandemic, and the world is in terror.

I pull on my work boots, take up the secateurs, the gloves and spade.

§

As I start to get my hands dirty, I know it's not just the garden in need of repair; it's me. Or at least, my spirit. What might be called my inner life is, like the space before me, half dead, fragmented, mouldy in some parts, dried out in others. Unbalanced, malnourished, filled with dispiriting mess.

Throughout the day's work, ripping out dead plants, forking compost through the powdery old soil, making space for new growth, I think about this thing: the 'inner life'. What is it, really? Does it happen in the same place we're supposed to find our 'inner resources'? Does everybody have an inner life? Does it matter if we don't?

What I do know is that for artists and writers, an inner life is inseparable from our work. My writing mind is a home I return to, away from and beyond the limits of my physical world. And as the pandemic causes the latter to shrink and grow a lot more frightening, escape to the former seems more essential than ever.

There's a sense that, at a time like this, artists should have a more effortless entry than most to that interior space. We habitually spend a lot of time there, after all. When we have a work in progress on the page or the canvas or the piano, we're carrying on two lives at once—one in the real world, another in the imagination. Quite often the inner world has a largeness of scope and sense of possibility that the outer world lacks. At this point in history, as everything in the real world closes down, that difference seems even starker.

This is not to say that it's only artists who have rich inner lives, of course. Anyone who attends thoughtfully to their personal domain—their interests and surroundings, the people they love, their work—already has an abundant interior world. And while your inner life and mine might be very different, I'd speculate that, at their most fulfilling, they might share some common traits.

One of these might be an attentiveness to the *concept* of the mind itself as something of value, something to be cared for and exercised, fed and challenged. This is an apprehension of the mind as a place of freedom and beauty, not to be damaged or filled with rubbish. With effort, it's a place that might be filled with a quiet, humming energy and yet remain peaceful—like a garden, wild and sheltered at once.

My own inner life needs structure and clarity, as well as moments of unruliness, to truly flourish. Any garden needs planning, boundaries, patience. It needs protection from invaders and at the same time acceptance of constant change. It knows that beauty takes time to show itself, that cherished inhabitants may die while other gifts appear as 'volunteers', those self-seeded surprises that just arrive and put down roots. A *magnificent* garden, though, like any work of art, is bolder in expression. It takes risks, is prepared to sacrifice, to fail and begin again. It's visionary, introducing new ideas, making improbable—but exciting—connections.

When I'm immersed in creative work, time expands and everything else drops away—the neediness and strain, the depletion and fragmentation that pervades so much of contemporary life. But that immersion doesn't happen easily, for in the Western world ordinary existence seems purposely designed to kill every aspect of the inner life. Capitalism, which rules all of us, depends on relentless productivity and expansion twinned with their opposite: unceasing, completely passive consumption.

Even now, as we claim greater appreciation of things that matter, like literature and meditation and cooking and wellness and music and art, for many of us it's really just a posher form of indiscriminate consumption. In our anxiety we're shovelling it all in, grabbing and discarding, mindlessly cramming one 'meaningful' thing and then another into every available space in ourselves and our days in the same rampantly acquisitive way we've always done.

At least I have. In these early pandemic months, I've watched myself seize upon novels and songs and yoga classes and recipes, gorge on them and then force them on others, pointing and urging, scarfing down all the 'mindfulness' I can before moving ahead, voracious as a locust. It might look like reading or meditating or cooking or connecting, but much of it has been mere displacement activity, the manifestation of sheer panic. And panic might be what capitalism loves best: production and consumption demand constant movement, constant noise.

When I consider the possibility of stopping all this—of simply going still—I'm drenched in relief.

When I *actually* stop, though, it's not as restful as that sounds. Stillness is a potentially creative space, but it is also scary. When first learning to meditate, we're sent into a state of alarm. For most of us, stillness gives rise to dread. Yet in those times my imaginative world has been most alive, I've learned something that feels important: stillness is not a void; it's a well. If I let it, it will fill itself. I can return to it again and again, and it will offer me something to draw upon in moments of crisis.

I suspect this paradoxical fear of and need for emptiness is why artists have always been such enthusiastic walkers. It's a useful trick: silent walking allows the mind to empty without the paralysing fear of stillness. A letting-go takes place. An easy, featherweight attention must be paid to the material world of the kerb, the footpath, the pedestrian crossing, which then allows the ethereal, invented world to expand inside the mind. This imaginative growth—without hope, without fear, without despair—is the precious fruit of the inner life.

There are many threats to a flourishing inner world other than constant motion. Illness, madness, poverty. Threats like living with someone who wants to crush you—break your bones, your optimism, your spirit. Or like fighting for your human rights in a society that doesn't want you to have them. Or working a job that, on some level, demands that you lie about who you are. The threats of exhaustion, distraction and fear, the eternal enemies of art making.

But even if our basic needs of safety, nourishment, rest and love are met, artists can still express a kind of terror about what they're doing. For a long time, I carried around with me this remark by Patrick White: 'I am constantly meeting ladies who say, "how lovely it must be to write", as though one sat down at the *escritoire* after breakfast, and it poured out like a succession of bread and butter letters, instead of being dragged out, by tongs, a bloody mess, in the small hours.'

Why did I like this statement so much, with its snobbery, its sneering at *ladies*? Because I recognised it. I know the cold metal of those tongs, I thought. I know those hours. I greeted it with the same gut-clenching recognition I did Nicholson Baker's chronically procrastinating poet, Paul Chowder, in *The Anthologist*. When Chowder's exasperated girlfriend finally begs him to 'Just go up there and write it!', Chowder says: 'I couldn't write it, it was too awful, too huge, it was like staring at death.'

Creativity as violent birth, as approaching death—this is absurd melodrama. Of course it is. And yet . . . at times my writing process has been so full of darkness that descriptions like these are the only ones that come close to the truth. I know I'm not alone in this experience, or in the great weariness that accompanies it. And I know I'm not the only artist to question the point of it all—to ask why on earth a sane person would keep *doing this* to herself. I grew so very tired of being afraid.

I was decades into writing books when I came across a psychology study that changed my life. It was a meta-analysis of 25 years of research into the most creative mood states. This analysis found that three central elements were common to experiences of profound creativity. They were a 'positive hedonic tone' or affect; a slightly elevated 'activation' or energy level; and a 'promotion focus'—in which the creator works with intent to seek gain rather than avoid pain. No surprise then that severe agitation, anger, anxiety—my closest companions!—were associated with the least creative mind state.

After reading this, I experimented. I began consciously trying to alter my mood before sitting down to a writing day. I practised flipping my usual bleak, nervy fear into a state of lightly excited, curious optimism. For some time, I faked it and then, haltingly,

I made it. I put the Patrick White quotation away, and my writing life slowly changed.

I began to conceive of my hours at the desk as a strangely beautiful circus tent inside which, only once the weights of self-loathing and derision were set down on the ground outside it, and only if I was attentive and observant and quiet, I could watch mesmerising things unfold. I learned that preparing my mind before sleep at night would more likely yield good things the next day. I found a deep, rich joy returning to my work.

Even if I forget all of this every single week and must constantly work my way back to it (why? *why* do I revert, always, to fear?), it's still this state of curious optimism that brings progress—sometimes even revelation. It's this state that allows the sinking into silence, and the profound peace of creative attention that opens up inside me. It's this state that lets time expand.

It makes space, too, for bravery and risk. The necessity of risk is one of the reasons spending indiscriminate time online is the greatest poison for my own inner world. I feel my courage seeping away with every emphatic opinion I scroll past, all of them revealing my own awkwardly forming ideas as incorrect and flimsy. That draining of courage is the signal to shut the garden gates and return to the work of composting and watering, at least until my own seedling can stand without support. Then it will be time to let the weather in, to shape and prune, to weed out imprudence or vanity or untruth. But until then, in this muddy germination phase when obscurity and *un*knowing are nourishment, sovereignty over the inner world must be absolute.

But enough of threats. What might *feed* a prosperous inner life?

Quite a lot from the outer life, it turns out. For me, it's best when there's a level of tranquillity in my physical surroundings. A cleanish house. Fresh food in the fridge, exercise, frequent contact with nature. A lot of early nights and early mornings. I've always loved that command attributed to Flaubert: 'Be regular and orderly in your life like a bourgeoise, so that you may be violent and original in your work.' If I can maintain even a shred of bourgeois order, it helps.

Like many writers, I'm obsessed by descriptions of other artists' working routines. Take Susan Sontag, who wrote endearingly equivocal lists of rules, complete with allowable exceptions, to help maintain her version of bourgeois order:

Starting tomorrow—if not today:

I will get up every morning no later than eight.
(Can break this rule *once* a week.)

I will have lunch only with Roger.
('No, I don't go out for lunch.' Can break this rule once every two weeks.)

I will write in the Notebook every day.
(Model: Lichtenberg's *Waste Books*.)

I will tell people not to call in the morning, or not answer
the phone.

I will try to confine my reading to the evening.
(I read too much—as an escape from writing.)

I will answer letters once a week.
(Friday?—I have to go to the hospital anyway.)

I make similar lists of rules, then I break them, then make them
again. It's something to do with maintaining a consoling sense of
order around the essential chaos of the creative process. Even when
the rules don't exactly work, aspiring to them helps.

Paradoxically, unfilled time—the one essential that should be
most available when everything's cancelled and travel even across
town is prohibited—seemed in shortest supply in the middle of the
pandemic. Hypervigilance, terror of uncertainty and that stillness
phobia threw many of us into a frenzy of overscheduling. For a time,
I was that Italian guy in the meme, trying to cram in yet another
appointment between the online yoga and Pilates, the Zoom drinks
and meetings, the chat rooms and podcasts and classes, the virtual
festivals, the endless talking, talking, talking.

But once I calmed down enough to recognise all this, I realised I had a choice: to step back, go inwards. Of course, this meant I was fortunate. I was safe, had no children to homeschool nor elderly parents to worry about. I had good health and people to love. My partner's business survived, after all. And despite the cancelled book tours and events, my own job was really no more precarious than it'd ever been. I had the resources for basic good citizenship—obeying safety rules, the various small economic and political acts incumbent upon those with power to support those without—and still some left over to devote to my inner world, my work.

Which brings me to one last precious nutrient for the life of the mind: joy.

So many in our world live in the midst of unspeakable pain, and as individuals we have no way of easing most of it. But it feels important to say that, despite this, we're allowed to protect and nurture that which helps each of us to live fully. Soon we'll die, but right now we're alive—let's not waste that outrageous luck. We have a right to joy.

It's sunset now. The garden is fed and pruned and mulched, the pavers swept, new seedlings in the ground. All that's needed from here is everything we already have: the autumn sunshine, a little rain, and time to let it grow.

2

The Getting of Wisdom

Finding your own teachers

When will I stop feeling like a beginner?

This question used to plague me about my work. When would I gain some confidence? At what point would I finally know how to do it? Practice is supposed to make progress, if not perfect, but each time I began a new book I was filled with the certain knowledge that I had no idea how to proceed. Nine books in, I still feel this way.

This is not an original observation—many writers say every new book sends them back to bewilderment—but it took me a long time to realise that, despite its inherent anxieties, this horrible state of *unknowing* was not a sign things were going badly, but rather indicated that I was on the right track. Philip Roth described this as 'looking for trouble'. Real problems arose, he said, 'not because the writing is difficult, but because it isn't difficult enough. Fluency can be a sign that nothing is happening . . . while being in the dark from sentence to sentence is what convinces me to go on.'

The solitary artist struggling in the dark, fumbling towards the light. While I recognise the fundamental truth of this lone struggle, it's also an image I want to resist, because the idea that complete isolation is a permanent necessity is also a lie, helping promote some destructive mythologising about the artist's natural state. For every solitary genius waiting for a personal illuminating flash, there are a great many solitary non-geniuses growing lonelier and more creatively stagnant by the darkening hour. Sometimes I think the high rates of depression and anxiety among writers—and they are high—are helped along by the pernicious myth that to be any good you must always work in desolate isolation.

It's one of many damaging ideas about creativity we've been fed for generations, largely by the patriarchy. Women's art making has always been more porous than most men's to the outside world. Male geniuses have had women to cook their food, raise their children and do their laundry (hello, Thoreau) while, like working women every-where, female artists have done all that and made their own work too. This could be why I have such an aversion to the word 'muse'—I've almost never heard women artists talk about muses, which bring to mind images of winsome girls, decorative and docile slaves to the towering male art figure. Art history is strewn with talented 'muses' whose own creativity was subsumed and diminished by that of their more famous lovers. It makes me so sad to think of all that unexplored potential, all that Great Art unmade, overlooked, abandoned.

But porousness in itself need not necessarily harm the work, nor subtract from one's pleasure in making it. On the contrary, in my experience. Many of the most profound moments of my creative life have come in talking about the process with fellow practitioners, in learning and sharpening my craft in company with others and, after a certain point, exposing my draft work to the generous but critical reading minds of selected peers.

Actors regularly take classes throughout their careers, and painters visit each other's studios to show and discuss their work in progress, so it's a mystery to me why many writers are so leery of this kind of openness. More than once, when I've mentioned to an established writer (and not only men, it must be said) that I've asked a writing friend to read a draft, or I've taken up a residency where I talk about work in progress, or enrolled in a masterclass or retreat, they've looked at me in horror and said, 'Oh, I could *never* do that.'

I've never had the guts to ask why not, so I don't know where this disdain comes from. Is it disdain? Sometimes it's just snootiness, I think—the belief that a skilled practitioner should have moved beyond such baby stuff as going to writing class. At other times, I've had the sense they think learning from others is somehow cheating.

Perhaps they fear outside influence would contaminate their unique creative process. Or maybe they just need absolute privacy for the entire duration of a book in order that their imagination's delicate balloon can stay aloft—a need I understand and respect.

It's true there are risks in opening up the inner world to the external one, and the line between inspiring influence and malign interference can be blurry. But in my own work, I tend to hunger for guidance from the outside world. I've often completely changed tack in my approach because of a stray remark I've heard another artist make, and sometimes I wonder if this means I'm too skittish about my own work, too easily bored or distracted to settle properly. I wonder if my constant search for new ways of working is a mark of dependence on others, or an immature restlessness, stopping me from uncovering the deeper truths that might be there if I delve further into what seems at first like the same old technical ground.

That may all be true. But as novelist Michelle de Kretser has written, 'Competence is the enemy of art.' And at this point in my writing life, I seek out instruction because the danger is not that my well-oiled way of working might be disrupted; it's that it might never be disrupted again. Interference with my process, in other words, is exactly what I want.

The trouble with ordinary writing classes, though, is that they tend to be built for the early years of development and then repeat the same material. There isn't much instruction specifically designed for artists with two or three decades of experience, which is why I've been inclined to invent the sort of 'classes' I want. Sometimes this has meant asking my peers to teach me what they know—to gather a group of mates together for a day, employing one to give the rest of us a masterclass in whatever they choose. Even if we're all at the same 'level' (whatever that means), and even when I'm sure I know all this stuff already, every single class has provoked a new idea, or reminded me of something I'd forgotten that now blazes with sudden urgency. On finishing each book, a writer is a different person, after all, and the old rules no longer necessarily apply.

At other times, my improvised tutorials have taken the shape of formal, structured conversations with other artists. I started a magazine of interviews with writers, which eventually became a book, then morphed into occasional workshops, then a podcast. After a while I began turning to other art forms as often as writing, and those allied-arts conversations have in recent times proved the most revelatory. Painters, playwrights, sculptors, filmmakers, actors, composers—even scientists, even builders, anyone who makes something appear where nothing was before—all have something to offer the writer about creativity. For one thing, they speak about their work in completely different terms, and this alone often brings fresh surprises about the writing process. A painter might talk of 'density' or 'refraction', and suddenly I'm aware of a new structural possibility for my novel in progress. A scientist speaks of pattern finding, but also the requirement to test and verify the pattern's solidity, and I realise I need to press harder on a recurring motif to test its strength. An actor tells me her work begins with a suspension of judgement, or points out the different body sites in which a person might carry their energy, and I have new insight into how I might enliven a character or, indeed, sustain a whole book. The accretion of these lessons over time has offered me much richer depth and scope than I can find in any writing manual.

When I later return to one of these conversations in print or podcast, I can chart the progress of the book I was writing by the questions I asked at the time, and by the tone of my response to their answers in the moment. Sometimes I wonder whether I could write at all without the transformative jolts these conversations have given me.

I think the solitary genius might say that reading and living should teach a writer everything they need to know. And they'd be right. But crucial discoveries about my work have also taken place in the intelligent, inquiring company of others. The paradox I've learned is this: every artist must protect and obey their own peculiar instincts—and, simultaneously, those very instincts must be constantly challenged and refreshed and developed.

Now I'm deep in the mess of my ninth book, that old question *must I always know nothing?* no longer haunts, but consoles. It's an invitation to discovery, to exploration, to lower yourself into the dark to mine for riches. Sometimes you can move into that darkness in the company of your weird, happy, melancholy, curious crew of fellow makers. You travel together until the openings of your separate tunnels appear and then you set off alone into yours, calling words of encouragement and solidarity to each other now and then. And under the floating sounds of those calls, in the soft lamplight of that comradeship, into your tunnel's earth you dig.

3

The Grumpy Struggle, Despair and the Luminous Solution

Nine kinds of creative thinking

The path into a book as you write it is a shadowy one. It's for this reason that so many of us take an avid—in my case, possibly slightly obsessive—interest in others' working methods. I read interviews with writers for inspiration, consolation and illumination. I was particularly taken by American author Janet Burroway's summary. 'Once I'm working', she has written, 'the process is much the same in every genre: the effort to get myself to the computer, a period of grumpy struggle, despair, the luminous solution that appears in bed or bath, joyful work; repeat; repeat; repeat.'

The grumpy struggle, despair, the luminous solution—how elegant and accurate a description of this slow emergence of a work of literature.

While my own expertise in matters of craft has grown substantially through the many years of my apprenticeship, my basic generative method has remained surprisingly unchanged. The first drafts of my novels develop from a series of discoveries made through what Helen Garner has described as 'scrub bashing'—instinctively pushing out through story, scene by often-unrelated scene. Invariably, these new discoveries see previous assumptions about various aspects of the work dropping away, and new possibilities taking their place.

Many of my most significant breakthroughs result from a growing sense that something's gone wrong with the work so far, followed by different attempts, using randomly chosen methods, to first identify and then solve the problem.

I've often compared the early stages of writing a book to the efforts of a sculptor with a lump of clay, gradually working away at it to discover the shape of a book—except that the writer must first invent their clay. And it can't be any old clay, it must be exactly the right clay for this work, this time.

During my doctoral studies years ago I came across some research that interested me greatly. It turned out that my sense of something being wrong, and the need to first invent the clay before I could begin to shape it, fitted rather tidily with established models of creativity. The first step of John Dewey's 1910 five-point model of creativity, for example, is 'a difficulty is perceived or felt', leading to the problem's definition and solution in subsequent steps. This initial sense of difficulty is also a key concept in what's known in the field as 'problem-finding'.

The concept of problem-finding was conceptualised in a landmark study by Jacob Getzels and Mihaly Csikszentmihalyi in 1976. (You may know Csikszentmihalyi as the author of the immensely popular books on the concept of 'flow' for creative and personal happiness.) Getzels and Csikszentmihalyi recruited more than 30 visual art students for an experiment. They gathered the artists in a room with a number of tables, on which were 27 different objects used in drawing classes. The students were told to choose some of the objects and use them to make a still life.

The researchers noticed two broad approaches to the task. The first group took a few objects and quickly got to work. The second took much longer to begin. They looked at objects, picked them up and put them down, rearranged them several times, and were generally slower in thinking about the arrangement of the things before they began work. Once they started, they also took longer to complete their drawings. Getzels and Csikszentmihalyi interpreted this as the first group trying to immediately solve a problem, and the second group as trying to find or create a problem before they began, then solving it through the art-making process.

A group of independent art experts then assessed the quality of the resulting works. The problem-finders' drawings scored much higher for creativity than the problem-solvers'. A decade later, in a follow-up study, around half the entire group had given up making art altogether. But of the half still working as professional artists, almost all of them came from the second group, the problem-finders. A further decade on, the quality of their work was still judged superior.

Getzels concluded: 'It is in fact the *discovery and creation of problems* rather than any superior knowledge, technical skill, or craftsmanship that often sets the creative person apart from others in his field.'

He later elaborated that a problem's resolution came from the way it was posed in the first place.

Prior to [a creative problem's] emergence there is no structure and no task; there is nothing to solve. After the problem emerges, the skills of the artist take over; control and ordering begin. [But] the crucial cognitive step is how the formless situation where there is no problem to solve . . . is transformed into a situation where a problem for solution emerges.

The formless situation where there is no problem to solve—otherwise known to writers, perhaps, as the blank page, that place of so much doubt and anxiety. The place where a creative problem is eventually found.

But what exactly is 'a creative problem' as opposed to any other kind? Another pair of researchers, Michael Mumford and Sigrid Gustafson, provided a useful four-part definition in 2012.

The first feature of a creative problem, they proposed, is that it is 'ill-defined'. Its goals and objectives are unclear, and the information needed to address these is not immediately available. Second, the problem must also be 'novel'—it has not existed as a problem before, and cannot be solved using available knowledge; knowledge must be re-formed and reshaped to create new ways of addressing the problem. Third, creative problems are 'complex'—they are multifaceted, may have a number of different solutions, and each of those solutions is quite different from the others. Finally, a creative problem is 'demanding'—the solution is not immediately clear, it can only be found by the individual, and, importantly, 'multiple cycles of problem-solving activities are required' before it can be solved. A 'progressive refinement' of a problem must take place in order to solve it.

When I read this research it was instantly clear that these characteristics—ill-defined, new, complex and demanding—were also the characteristics, for me, of an unwritten novel. And while working artists are generally unfamiliar with (and, frankly, probably uninterested in) this sort of terminology, I've found that many nevertheless explicitly allude to problem-finding as an essential—if not *the* essential—part of their personal creative process.

I've already referred to Roth's looking-for-trouble approach, and his assertion that fluency isn't as comforting as one would assume. In fact, at the start of writing a book, he told the *Paris Review*, 'what matters most isn't there at all. I don't mean the solutions to problems, I mean the problems themselves.'

New Zealand novelist Lloyd Jones also believes in the necessity of difficulty. He told me in an interview that his work in progress at the time was 'problematic', but this was a familiar situation.

> I get a bit caught up in trying to reject the conventions of narrative, which pushes me out into an area where it doesn't work, and then that kind of redirects me back to where I probably should have been all the way along . . . The starting point is often artificial, and that's probably where dissatisfaction sits, and pushes you into a territory where you have to take more imaginative risks . . . It's almost like every time I set out on a writing project I'm learning how to write all over again.

For Jones, being pushed into a difficult space and having to find his way out seems to be a prerequisite for good work.

The American photorealist painter Chuck Close is even more explicit. He's told more than one interviewer that getting himself 'into trouble' is a key necessity for his work.

For me, the most interesting thing is to back yourself into your own corner where no one else's answers will fit. You will somehow have to come up with your own personal solutions to this problem that you have set for yourself because no one else's answers are applicable . . . I think our whole society is much too problem-solving oriented. It is far more interesting to [do] 'problem creation' . . . ask yourself an interesting enough question and your attempt to find a tailor-made solution to that question will push you to a place where, pretty soon, you'll find yourself all by your lonesome—which I think is a more interesting place to be.

After reading this research and other studies I shifted gear, taking my personal interest in writers' working methods into a more formal investigation. I conducted a small longitudinal study of the cognitive processes of creativity as they played out among a group of writers I knew. I've met with these writers regularly for more than twenty years. Such a group will be familiar to many people in any field—the fellow practitioners you meet with now and then to commiserate with, chat about work and discuss your latest professional tussles.

The writers in this particular group don't share their work itself as it is made, but they certainly discuss it at length, laying out the issues and process, asking each other questions, offering potential solutions, celebrating successes, sympathising over disasters.

I guessed that I might be able to harvest some useful information from the group's ordinary conversations, to explore problem-finding and other processes in more depth. They cheerfully agreed to take part, allowing me to record our meetings over the course of nine months. Our talk took place as usual in all its chaotic, digressive, random-seeming form—the only difference was my phone on the table recording our chat, and the phone was soon forgotten and certainly ignored. My job then was to analyse the transcripts, to look for commonalities in the approaches we took to our writing. After much listening and sifting and coding, I found that we were indeed repeatedly using a shared series of specific creative processes, almost always without knowing it.

In the end I identified nine methods that we used to find, and then solve, the problems of our books. I then looked to interviews with other writers and discovered that very often they, too, articulated these same practices. I categorised and named the processes as follows: heat-seeking; drilling, digging and diving; connecting and merging; circling and cycling; disrupting or overturning; impersonating or embodying; territory-mapping; forecasting and hypothesising; and, finally, waiting or suspending.

Some will be immediately familiar to any artist reading this, but others may be more surprising. The processes can occur at any stage, often repeatedly and quite arbitrarily through the art-making process, and not all of them need to be used to produce a final work. What follows is an exploration of each of these processes in a little detail.

HEAT-SEEKING is the way artists separate promising from unpromising material by sensing and following the 'power' or 'energy' coming from any part of the work. Importantly, this energy can come from unexpected places, and often seems to sort of glow at a writer from one corner of the work while they're focused on another seemingly more relevant or important part.

Heat-seeking is often spoken of in terms of whether draft material is 'alive' or 'dead'. Dead material won't lead to new possibilities. 'Living' material, on the other hand, even if emitting only the weakest pulse, can be developed further.

Other words my writers used for this heat were 'goodness', 'movement', 'life', 'urgency', 'spark', 'ignition'. Anything that quickened the interest of the writer when they thought of it, whether or not it made any rational sense at all, was a signal that important material lay there.

While heat-seeking is a crucial process, it's important to note that work can still proceed in its absence. Indeed, working through very long stretches of 'dead' material is the normal experience of many artists as they seek out the essential energy (an aside: I'd suggest that many works are finished, produced and shown or published in which the artist has never actually found this energy).

Heat-seeking is the most important of all the nine techniques I discovered, and learning to trust one's instinct for it is vital. Without this capacity, artists may find themselves merely replicating the conceptual or stylistic work of others. But once an artist learns to pay close attention to where the real energy is coming from, a truly creative work of art can emerge.

DRILLING, DIGGING AND DIVING, the next process, describes a movement beyond the surface of comprehension to a deeper level of creative thought. It's often quite closely related to heat-seeking. The writers in my study commonly spoke of 'going deeper', showing the writing mind as something 'beneath', beyond or behind normal conscious thought. Other writers frequently use metaphors of darkness, and say their works come from 'underneath' places of gloom, haze or half-light: tunnels, wells, holes and ocean depths. Many see this digging and diving phase as a difficult, lonely and isolating time.

Importantly, as Janet Burroway signalled, the diving or digging must happen *repeatedly*, the artist often moving to a new level of inquiry each time. There's an understanding that material of serious worth is not easy to find and comes from a 'deep' place. Shallowness is, after all, associated with triviality; answers lying close to the surface are often seen to have little value.

CONNECTING AND MERGING is related to one of the accepted hallmarks of creative thinking: associative thought. This is the ability to plausibly connect concepts and ideas hitherto thought to be separate. The drive to connect seemingly disparate things is often instinctive rather than logical. The relationships are psychic and symbolic, and the experienced artist learns to trust the leaps of their own mind.

Novelist Richard Ford has often spoken of this joining of unlike things as one of the sources of his art, implying that the joining point, the ligature between them, is where the new revelations of art come from. Other artists discover that the connections are not forced, but rather have been there all the time, only revealed later in the process. Novelist Margaret Drabble put it this way:

It's nearly always unintentional. I look back at it and think, 'Oh, that relates to that.' When you're writing in a certain vein, everything grows out of the same source. Occasionally it's more deliberate . . . It's a natural associative process, really. It's not exactly symbolism, it's just how life is. You notice one thing and then you notice the same thing again tomorrow.

Sometimes, when I've been stuck on a patch of work, I'll try both of these approaches: forcing unlikely things together to see what the result looks like—which often leads to a new, quite natural connection—or simply looking very carefully at the disparate elements I have to see if there may already be plausible connections I've not noticed before.

CIRCLING AND CYCLING bears a relationship to the digging and diving described earlier. It refers to the way artists return, often almost neurotically, to material they've already created. It is sometimes deliberate and sometimes done with surprise, the writer finding themselves once more at an old idea but with new understanding.

Sometimes it's a kind of 'run-up' to creating new work—a technique Peter Carey called 'cantilevering' in his interview in the seminal Australian book on writing process, *Making Stories* by Kate Grenville and Sue Woolfe. He spoke of realising something is wrong, and the work beginning to feel 'shallow and false and unsatisfactory'. At such a point, Carey said, he would start again, writing all the way through and beyond the unsatisfactory part, until it once again grew shaky. He'd do this repeatedly, and in so doing uncover the real substance of what it was he was trying to find. Sometimes, he said, what was uncovered through this repetitive cantilevering eventually turned out to be the very heart of a book.

Necessary, profound discoveries about a work can come, then, from returning to the material and reworking it, revising and writing again, until a missing connection or a new development suddenly appears.

DISRUPTING OR OVERTURNING is a more conscious method, of opposition, in which an artist deliberately disrupts or 'messes up' existing work so as to create movement or change, or to provoke a revelation of meaning.

This disruptive process can involve a quite mechanistic 'reversal' or overturning of a previous approach, where a writer abandons an unsuccessful attempt or concept and literally tries doing the opposite. In my novel *The Natural Way of Things*, for example, I began by writing a realist story set in the past—but for many long months, the work was dead on the page. Not until I flipped the time frame to a possible future, and realism into a form of *sur*realism, did the work begin to come alive enough for me to continue with it.

The disruption process can also involve introducing some kind of 'wildness' or 'weirdness'—something unexpected—into the narrative, which in turn might create energy or more story. Importantly, this applies not only to the subject matter or content of the work, but can mean introducing unorthodoxies to its structure, style, tone or rhythm. One of my study participants memorably put it this way: 'When in doubt, do violence to the page.'

IMPERSONATING OR EMBODYING is the deliberate, imaginative borrowing of another's perspective as a useful creative tool. Artists do this in several ways. First, there's the commonplace influence we all experience in embracing and emulating another writer's style, technique or approach to form. This could mean seeking out a particular work as a structural or conceptual model, or returning to a favourite writer to examine how they might have composed their work, or just hearing about the creative process of others.

But there's another, more interesting and less conventional form of impersonation—that which comes from imagining the perspective offered by someone, or even some*thing*, completely unrelated to you or your work.

One participant in my study for a time took inspiration for her novel from the work of film director Baz Luhrmann. She was attracted to his audaciousness with pastiche and his seeming fearlessness in the face of critical failure, as well as, in her words, 'the wild boldness of the anachronistic mash-up'. During this time, she would quite deliberately attempt to see her work through her imagined version of Luhrmann's creative perspective. In conversation she would sometimes refer to 'Bazzing up' her work in progress: emboldening her approach and taking more risks, ignoring her fear of melodrama or theatricality.

In a similar fashion, I found comfort and inspiration in the disturbing and mysterious works of the surrealist artist and sculptor Louise Bourgeois. During the writing of *The Natural Way of Things*, I was often highly anxious that I didn't understand the meaning of what I was doing. When I came across Bourgeois's strange works, I decided to abandon my attempts to understand, by way of 'pretending' to be a visual artist. Rightly or wrongly, I felt visual artists were not required to articulate the meaning of their work as they made it in the way writers feel obliged to; it seemed to me that their job was purely to create.

In one recorded session, I articulated my impersonation process by alluding to Bourgeois's *Cell* installations, in which female body parts and pieces of clothing hang inside large, threatening metal cages:

Every time I start getting anxious, when I think, 'I don't know what it means, what am I trying to say?' and all that, I think, 'I'm just going to be a visual artist with this book.' I'm going to be Louise Bourgeois, who just made her weird things and put them out there—I'll just hang some uteruses in a cage. That's the only way for it to work.

One writer not only used other artists' imagined perspectives for inspiration, but other art *forms* altogether, especially theatre and painting. At one stage she found it helpful to conceive of her novel as a baroque painting: 'If I could, I would [make my book] a huge history painting, that wasn't like any history painting you've ever seen. With a massive frame, and maybe people climbing into and out of it.'

Using other art forms and artists as role models in this way can give a surge of energy to the writer's process, with great surprises and important developments often resulting.

TERRITORY-MAPPING is a way of assessing progress so far, often in the form of lists or 'maps' or diagrams, via which the immediate route ahead can be determined. Territory-mapping is often used to alleviate the anxiety stemming from the general chaos of art making, in which 'not knowing' is an essential element.

One of my participants wrote lists of key concepts, events and scenes already written, as well as some yet to be created. She noted: 'Instead of . . . feeling as if those key ideas or areas are an archipelago every time I've been away from the writing—that there are all these islands scattered out—now I've got this circumference around them for quick reference.'

Another used a water metaphor to describe her territory-mapping.

It's a bit like you're underwater when you're doing those early drafts. And then you can look up and see a bit of something— 'oh, there's a surface there'—and you stick your head out and you're looking all around. It's like you realise, 'I'm in a swimming pool this big, and there is the shore', so you have a sudden sense of the terrain. Whereas before that, you're just underwater, going 'which way is up?'

Territory-mapping, then, is a conscious, deliberate effort to gather draft material into one space, examine it as a whole (even if very little has actually been created), assess how much if any of it might be useful in generating further material, and prepare the way for the next stage. It can take place throughout the creative process for purposes of consolation, gathering strength, boosting morale or improving focus. But among my writers, territory-mapping was only used occasionally, and not often in the very early stages of a work. On occasion it serves not only as an organisational and evaluative tool but sometimes a generative one at the same time—an example of how one technique can often perform several functions at once.

FORECASTING AND HYPOTHESISING is a technique in which the writer posits as-yet-untested ideas for development of the work, both in a conceptual and sometimes a logistical sense, in order to proceed. It's related but oppositional to territory-mapping: where the latter is concerned with work already done, forecasting and hypothesising is a way of looking forwards to possibilities yet to emerge.

Sometimes it is a form of suggesting what is *likely* to happen—i.e. that the coming development is in some way inevitable—and at other times it is a vaguer, more actively speculative exercise, an expression of what 'could' happen in the future. This second form of speculation, guessing at what might or could develop in a story, can be a kind of investigative, aspirational or even brainstorming exercise.

In one conversation, for example, I shared a note I'd written to myself about what I wanted for my book, in its final form.

I want a lithe, lively quality to the writing. For the story to be surprising and intriguing but not bleak . . . I want it to run smoothly and quickly, and to be able to dip in and out of the past in smooth scoops . . . I want it to be relaxed, and true, and without any sense of strain or workmanship. I want the girls to be fun, still, somehow, despite what is happening to them. I want to capture what teenagehood is like—I fear I can't do this, but will try, somehow.

Forecasting and hypothesising incorporates both a highly pragmatic, almost logistical function—planning out daily or monthly schedules, for example, or listing 'jobs' to do within the work, such as joining slabs of material—and a more instinctive guessing at what might lie in wait for the writer. Both can be used at different times, and often simultaneously.

WAITING OR SUSPENDING, the final process in the list, is in one sense just an absence; indeed, it can resemble abandoning work altogether. However, it appears frequently in writers' talk as a purposeful decision to 'give up', 'let go', 'ignore' or 'stop caring' about a stage or part of the work proving troublesome. This is a decision to wait for meaning to reveal itself, to suspend judgement over the relevance or importance of an area of work, or just to 'worry about that bit later'.

Often this is a tack to take when one remains attracted to an area of work despite there being no rational reason to think it is important. Sometimes the decision to wait is made after an unsuccessful attempt at forcing progress. It's important to stress that one needs to earn the right to let go or abandon. If you're just opting out when things get tough, it's unlikely to yield anything interesting. But quite often, after struggling unsuccessfully but long and hard with an unworkable story, the decision to step back can allow a kind of cognitive relaxation that will bring forth the solution. This is what's meant by the 'incubation' phase in some models of creativity, where abandoning conscious effort can allow the percolation of ideas to go on and solutions to emerge of their own accord—'the luminous solution' arriving for Janet Burroway in the bath.

In *The Writing Life*, Annie Dillard famously wrote about sitting with the patient: 'I do not so much write a book as sit up with it, as with a dying friend. During visiting hours, I enter its room with dread and sympathy for its many disorders. I hold its hand and hope it will get better.'

Joan London has reported that completely abandoning work actually led to a significant breakthrough in her writing. When serious illness forced her to stop working after publishing some lauded story collections, the suspension was not only physical but psychic.

> It was time out. I didn't have to do anything. I didn't force myself. I didn't have any deadlines. I said, 'I've had enough. I've had enough of striving and of ambition and the literary world . . . I remembered that Rilke injunction: You must change your life. That's what really happened to me. It was a very solitary period of time off, of reading and thinking.

It was during this period of 'time off' that the central idea for London's first and much-lauded novel *Gilgamesh* came to her in a dream.

William Maxwell used the term 'actively passive' to describe his own waiting for material to arrive.

> I just hang over the typewriter waiting to see what is going to happen. It begins with the very first sentence. I don't will the sentence to come; I wait, as actively passive as I can possibly be . . . When I wrote those fables and sat with my head over the

typewriter waiting patiently, empty as a bucket that somebody's turned upside down, I was waiting for a story to come from what you could call my unconscious.

Contrary to the popular maxim that 'a writer writes', it is clear that quite often, and for different creative reasons, a writer *waits*.

§

I spent many months thinking about these discoveries, sorting and parsing them, enriched by the whole experience. But at the end of it all, after the research was completed and the doctorate finished and awarded, came that pesky and familiar and important question: So what? What does all this mean for the person sitting down before the blank page? Would knowing about any of this stuff—the problem-finding, the nine processes—help me become a better writer? Might it form some ballast against that perennial exhaustion, the toleration of endless uncertainty? Would it allow my work to come more easily?

Well, with the distance of several years, writing now from the middle of two novels later, the answer to those last anxious questions is: not really. But it has become a consoling diagnostic tool—when I'm in a bad patch, I can look at the list and think, *It's okay, I'm just in the suspension phase.* When the work is going very badly, even such small comfort as this is not to be dismissed. But while this and other creative cognition research may yield interesting ways of understanding how one's mind works or has worked in the past to create a book, I think in the end it doesn't help in the creation of a new work.

This could be a dispiriting realisation, but actually I find it cheering. Because the value of a new work of art lies in its mysterious, irreplicable nature. As so many writers have articulated, each book *must be* a never-before-experienced creative problem. At the start of each day, what we sit down with is the quiet space and the blank page. And there's no research or book or teacher who can help you at that moment: every artist must find their own way of tunnelling back into the subconscious, digging away, and then bringing what they find out into the light.

Right now I'm reading the journals and letters of Katherine Mansfield. The reason we write, Mansfield declared, is the 'anguish and rapture' . . . 'the moment when the act of creation takes place— the mysterious change—when you are no longer writing the book, *it* is writing, *it* possesses you'.

I'm romantic enough to believe that good art should somehow cost the maker, that the deepest satisfaction really is in the process, and that if you knew how to do it at the start, there would be no reason to proceed. And I'm also romantic enough to believe that without the grumpy struggle, sometimes even the despair, you don't earn Mansfield's moment of rapture. If an artist is reaching for something beyond what they know they can do, when a work is truly a deep and questing exploration, the joy when the connections are made and the thing finally resolves itself is all the more dazzling.

§

Much of what happens when a work is finished, once a book is sent into the world or a show to an exhibition or a production opens on the stage, is the opposite of creativity. There's a great anxiety attached to this period, for it feels as if so much is at stake—and not only for oneself. The people who love an artist, their professional supporters, their creative peers, everyone wants the work to succeed. But out there in the world it is measured, graded, evaluated and—often—damned to oblivion, and all of that happens in a realm completely beyond the artist's skill or control.

I think at such times it's helpful to remember that all this external measuring and grading is no part of an artist's job. Our energies must be dedicated, purely and simply, to the work itself—returning again and again to the studio and the blank space of the unformed work, defying the cold logic that says you are only worth how much money you earn or what others think of you. Showing up to that empty space with curiosity and courage is an exercise in the greatest freedom we can know—intellectual freedom, to explore your obsession with something nobody but you cares about, to pursue your own strange thoughts and dreams, to climb right inside your own dark wormhole of fascination and stay there.

On one very bad writing day a few years back, I thought again about giving up. I wrote to a couple of my writer friends.

Not going so well this week, after all. Somehow swamped again with the futility of this work, trying to find the point of writing a dark, bleak book about girls imprisoned and trapped and reviled. Yesterday I couldn't see how I was not just adding yet more ugliness to the world. But I have just bucked myself up a little bit by writing a list of reasons to keep going. Here's what I came up with.

- *To make something beautiful. Beauty does not have to mean prettiness but can emerge from the scope of one's imagination, the precision of one's words, the steadiness and honesty of one's gaze.*

- *To make something truthful. 'Beauty is truth, truth beauty.'*

- *To make use of what you have and who you are. Even a limited talent brings an obligation to explore it, develop it, exercise it, be grateful for it.*

- *To make, at all. To create is to defy emptiness. It is generous, it affirms. To make is to add to the world, not subtract from it. It enlarges, does not diminish.*

- *Because, as Iris Murdoch said, paying attention is a moral act. To write truthfully is to honour the luck and the intricate detail of being alive.*

I returned to that list for comfort often through the writing of my novel, but it has stayed with me in the years since because I think it speaks to the reasons we need art at all. It often feels that we've entered a new dark age—an age in which science is rejected in favour of superstition and greed, in which our planet is in desperate need of rescue, in which bigotry and religion are inseparable.

In the midst of this gloom, to create is an act of enlargement, of affirmation. It lights a candle in the darkness, offering solace, illumination—maybe even the possibility of transformation—not just for the maker but for the reader or viewer, which is to say all of us. Art urges us to imagine and inhabit lives other than our own, to be more thoughtful, to feel more deeply, to challenge what we think we already know. Art declares that we contain multitudes, that more than one thing can be true at once. And it gives us a breathing space, in which we can listen more than talk, where we can attentively question our own beliefs. It gives us a place in this chaotic world in which to find the sort of meaning that only arises out of the stillness, deep within our quiet selves.

4

Unconscious Bias

• — •

The dreaming mind

I had a weird dream last night. Don't worry, I'm not going to tell you about it. I'll tell you something else instead, about fairytales.

The fairytale I remember most vividly from childhood—or at least I thought I did—is 'The Girl Who Trod on the Loaf' by Hans Christian Andersen. This little-known story concerns a vain and haughty girl who, though very poor, possesses a single pair of exquisite shoes. In my memory of the tale, the girl's mother sends her with the family's last sixpence to buy a loaf of bread—the last food they can expect to eat before they starve. On her way home with the loaf, the girl comes to a puddle. Faced with a choice between muddying her beautiful shoes or the betrayal of her mother and starvation, she chooses the latter, casting the loaf of bread into the puddle to use as a stepping stone. But as soon as her foot touches the loaf the puddle becomes a terrifying vortex, wrenching her bodily through the mud, down, down into a hellish underworld. And that's where she remains, punished eternally for her vanity.

When I think of this story, I also think of a recurring nightmare that lasted throughout my childhood. The dream always began with my walking across the road from my real-life house to a neighbour's letterbox. In the dream, my opening of the letterbox lid was the starter signal for a dread-filled ritual in which I was snatched up by two vast, duelling universes (unending, dark and starry undulations of malevolent power, existing in a time and space far beyond our earth). Each time, I was transformed into a tiny ball which the two universes threw to each other in a game of catch, increasing the distance between them with each toss. The threat—terrifying but also, I knew, somehow magnificent—was twofold: either being destroyed by their malice as they threw and caught me, or being dropped, disappearing into the infinite void between them.

Why have I put these things together, the dream and the story?

I was drawn to the pages of that story repeatedly and inexorably, with the same dread-filled compulsion that sent me towards the letterbox in my dream. In both dream and story there was terror, and the exhilaration of surrendering to that terror. Each contained only a few stark images, but they still glitter in my mind with the same power they always had: white letterbox, starry darkness, silver ball. Red shoes, white bread, black mud. And annihilation.

The dream and the story shared something else, too: an intense privacy of experience, indescribable to anyone else, especially adults. Part of my dream's force was the invisibility of my terror to anyone else. I was merely a speck, a plaything in a game. Some of that threat— and the exhausting euphoria—always remained with me on waking; perhaps I feared it would leak right out into my conscious life if I spoke of it once morning came. Or, conversely, perhaps I feared it would dissolve into ordinariness if exposed to the light.

When I went back to find and reread the fairytale as an adult, I was surprised by two things: how short is the part in which the bread actually features in the story, and how long and detailed and gruesome is the description of the girl's penance in hell, where she is forced to become a statue, her feet glued to the bread, and where punishments she visited upon others in life return to torture her. On earth she had pulled the wings off flies, for example; in hell, a captive statue, she is doomed to endure those same wingless flies crawling over her face.

My memory of the girl's relationship with her mother has also proven hazy. In the story, the girl is raised by a wealthy family who feed and clothe her, and who try in vain to correct her 'proud and arrogant' character. It's when she's sent to visit her real mother with a gift of bread that she commits her atrocity at the puddle (this solves the puzzlement I always felt about how such a poor girl came by such dazzling shoes, though amusingly this was the only point of logic that bothered me). The story also has redemption. The girl remains in hell for generations, until one day an old woman on earth cries in pity for her—at which she suddenly becomes a bird and is magically released. I had no memory at all of this happy ending.

Adults often carry indelible memories of tales they read or were told as children, I've found. One friend's adored favourite story as a girl was 'Bluebeard'. (If you can't recall or don't know it, suffice to say it climaxes with a young wife's discovery of the bloody corpses of her many slaughtered predecessors garlanding the walls of her husband's locked chamber.) Another friend's favourite was a story involving a bear whose parents were killed. He remembers nothing else about the story but this, and his desire to experience the horror of it over and over again. None of us remembered the stories' cheery conclusions. Nor do we recall any parental concern at our gruesome tastes, if indeed they were ever noticed.

I wonder if the fact that we often heard these tales before bedtime helped give them their potency. Perhaps taking those images into our sleep somehow rooted them in the unconscious so deeply they would never fade away.

When we think 'fairytale', we tend to think of the most famous ones, with stories that proceed in some logical form. Even if it's a stretch that a wolf could convincingly masquerade as a grandmother,

'Little Red Riding Hood' has a beginning, a middle, a logical climax and ending. So does 'Goldilocks and the Three Bears', or 'Hansel and Gretel'. Maybe we know these tales so well because they're easy to follow and illustrate and so have lasted, passed down through the generations.

But a flick through some of the lesser-known fairytales shows a roiling unpredictability and shapelessness that can only be compared to dreams. The tales of the Brothers Grimm and Hans Christian Andersen are full of absurd and irrelevant phenomena that suddenly appear and disappear—like piles of talking 'dead fingers' or squabbling shovels and brooms—that imprint themselves briefly on the main story and then vanish completely. Many of the stories, like 'The Girl Who Trod on the Loaf', linger seemingly forever in strange narrative byways and then abruptly end, without clarity or logical resolution.

All of this, to me, echoes the formlessness of dreaming and sudden waking.

Maybe it's silly to take dreams as seriously as I do, to be so susceptible to their loose, disconnected, somehow talismanic imagery. Other writers certainly pay a lot of attention to sleep, though. Many observe that when their work is going well they begin to dream about the people and events and scenes of their books. Artists are often insomniacs, as well as frequent nappers, which may or may not be related. Some writers speak of wanting to shrink the space between sleep and work, starting as soon as possible after waking in an attempt to stay in a liminal zone between dreaming and conscious thought. Joan Didion has said that when she's nearing the end of a book, she needs to 'sleep in the same room as it . . . Somehow the book doesn't leave you when you're asleep right next to it.'

I'm one of the nappers, usually when my conscious mind is trying to flee a problem on the page. I'm often overwhelmed by a kind of narcolepsy, but only on a writing day, and only when I've hit some impasse in my work. At those times I give in and fall into a short but deep sleep, waking after 20 or 30 minutes to move straight to the desk, a useful sentence having formed itself in my unconscious mind and now waiting to be written down. This is why I like to have a bed in my writing room if I can, wherever I am. I've seen daybeds in plenty of artists' studios, too, and felt consoled that I'm not alone in using sleep as both escape from and solution to working problems.

There are lots of theories about why we dream: dreams work to lay down our memories, or they're a form of unconscious therapy, soothing the intensity and hurt of difficult waking experiences. Or they have no purpose at all—they're just stray electrical impulses flinging about random thoughts and images from the brain, and our ability to construct dream 'stories' on waking is merely an attempt to make sense of the senseless.

I heard a neuropsychologist say that dreams arise from a part of the brain he rather poetically called 'the wanting system', a seeking or reward system. There was a possibility, he speculated, that the function of dreams was to allow one to safely act out experimental, potentially dangerous or crazy impulses. If the bizarre imagery of dreams were to surface during waking hours, it would lead to mental instability and chaos, he said, but dreams could offer a kind of virtual-reality system, a way of trying out a behaviour or scenario (flying, for example) without the real-world penalty of actually doing it.

The wanting system. Sometimes it certainly feels like that. Like everyone else, I've had euphoric flying or swimming dreams, and I dream often of reuniting with lost people—my parents returning from the dead, or a friend from the wreckage of a painful falling-out. Our anxiety dreams of public failure or death or other catastrophe must come from this place too, except from the opposite, un-wanting direction. When you wake up sobbing real tears from dreams of a spouse dying, or your father returning to life and then leaving *again*, it's hard to see such strong emotion as mere neurochemical sawdust, even if that's what it is.

Some writers are as intrigued as I am by dreams, and some deliberately turn to them as sources and fuel for their work. 'I do a lot of work in dreams,' novelist Rodney Hall, who describes himself as an expressionist, told an audience recently. It takes practice to gain conscious entry to your dream life, Hall said, but he'd learned from the renowned British writer Robert Graves that the first step was to abandon any attempt to interpret them, which would be to 'tamper' with and destroy their force. The way to record a dream, Hall went on, is not to try to retain the whole but, as soon as one wakes, to take a notebook from the bedside and 'write down a minimum of three but preferably four key things in the dream'. Later, this would help him to recover as much of it as would be useful. For him, a recent example had been a way to connect the previously troublesome unlinked strands of his novel—the solution revealed in a dream.

Hearing someone else's dream in its entirety can indeed quickly grow dull, but I've sometimes remembered images from other people's dreams for years. And having a highly vivid dream life myself, I've always been irritated by the widely accepted prohibition on dreams in fiction. 'Tell a dream, lose a reader,' Henry James is supposed to have said, possibly apocryphally. But when dreaming is such an important part of so many inner lives, it seems odd—even a kind of lie—for fiction to pay it no attention or pretend it doesn't happen.

I do understand why fictional dreams are frowned upon; we all know how boring and meaningless our dreams are to others, no matter how fascinating they might be to us. But I'm always gratified when a writer breaks this rule, as Helen Garner did in her classic novel *Monkey Grip*, which is filled with detailed accounts of narrator Nora's dreams. Partly I like the simple truthful mess of them, and Garner's trust in the reader to take an interest in every meander of Nora's psyche. It's consistent with Garner's trademark willingness to expose the private, unmediated, uncontrolled self—the very thing that has drawn admiring readers to her work for so long. Take that, Henry.

There is, though, one compelling reason to leave dreams out of fiction, and that is the impossibility of *inventing* a convincing dream. The conscious mind, or mine at least, can't help but try to impose some narrative or semi-rational order on the invented dream's images or events. A made-up dream so often lacks the deep chaos or mystery of a real one, and the result is a ploddingly obvious—and needless—telegraphing of an internal malaise.

Still, the fact that the images and moods of real dreams can linger in my mind and my body for days or sometimes years convinces me that they're too important to leave out of books altogether. When it's done effectively, even a fragment of dream in a novel can offer a flicker of the unknown, the uncanny, signalling that rational thought is not the only realm where meaning can be found.

If I'm honest, I also find a simple adolescent pleasure in bucking the rules, even if the only one who notices is me. I loathe being told what's 'allowed' or not in art, and even if this defiance of accepted convention doesn't always work, I always admire the artist who obeys nobody and nothing but herself.

I've begun to rebel against the dream ban in my own novels by writing in traces of my real-world dreams, or at least acknowledging that the people in my books understand their unconscious lives to have meaning and value. In *The Weekend*, one character expresses it this way:

> At times she felt on the edge of discovering something very important—about living, about the age beyond youth and love, about this great secret time of a person's life. But she had not uncovered it yet, though it seemed to flourish in her dream life, which was an underground river of rich, vibrant meaning, flowing beneath her days. She knew this now, that it was not just your brain resting, but a whole life being lived . . .

In or outside of books, dreams remind us that no matter how much we pretend otherwise, we're not in full command of our lives. They remind us that cause and effect are not the solid truths we perceive them to be, that mess and unruliness are always present outside or beneath what's visible. A remembered dream is a message from the unconscious to say that however much we try, we never really know ourselves at all.

The work of artists is to welcome this unknowing, to allow that the spaces between things—between, say, a dream and a fairytale placed side by side—contain mystery and significance, not just emptiness.

The poet Anne Sexton said of writing: 'To be a fool, that perhaps requires the greatest courage.' My dream life shows me every morning that I am a fool, and that a good life in this world requires the courage and the grace to know it. Making art is an attempt to bring into cohesion the fragmented, lost parts of ourselves and our world. And the dream's mad symbols—its bright letterbox, its tiny silver ball, its shapeless dark—remind me that while any such attempt is surely doomed, it's still a beautiful thing, to try.

5

Take an Object

•————————•

How art can transfigure hatred

A couple of days after Trump's electoral victory in 2016, a fresh piece of graffiti appeared on a fence in a middle-class, gentrifying suburb of Melbourne. In foot-high, almost elegant cursive lettering, stark white on a smooth black panel, it said: *1. Cunt-punch a slut.*

When I saw it, I felt dead inside. I turned away. I tried to put it from my mind; failed. It kept returning, white on black. A stark, hateful statement of the new world order.

I soon realised that this inner deadness was familiar, for it was the same kind of psychic collapse I'd felt on first hearing the radio documentary that lit the fuse for my novel *The Natural Way of Things*.

The documentary was about the Hay Institution for Girls, a brutal prison for teenaged girls which operated in the rural Australian town of Hay in the 1960s and 70s. At this state-run prison for young women deemed somehow wayward or promiscuous, the inmates were put to hard labour, forced to march everywhere in military fashion, forbidden from speaking to one another. At all times they had to look at the ground. The authorities played many twisted psychological games—like ordering the girls to build a stone paving path and then, on its completion, smash it to pieces—as official, sanctioned punishments. But there were also many sadistic unofficial penalties. In a place full of young women 'guarded' almost entirely by men who despised them, you can imagine the horrors inflicted.

When the radio program ended, I wanted only to forget this appalling place and what it meant. But what I'd heard, and the images of those girls, would not leave me. What seemed cruellest of all was this: the reason many of the girls were first imprisoned was that they'd been sexually molested in some way—at home, in the community— and they'd *told someone about it*. It was speaking about what had happened, and asking for help, that got them locked up.

Slowly and reluctantly, I understood I had a compulsion to write about this. I began work on a realist novel about a prison for young women, set in a remote part of Australia in the 1970s. But a pressing problem quickly emerged: the writing was dreadful. The characters were lifeless clichés; nothing on the page surprised. The inner deadness I'd felt on hearing what the real girls suffered had spread to my language, to the sentences and the story, and my imagination could not revive them.

It was around this time that two truths came to me: realism was not going to help me this time, and the material, the substance of this book, could not remain neatly in the past, for I'd begun to notice fleeting news items involving young women. A publicist took legal action against the chief executive of a department store who preyed on and harassed her sexually. A female army cadet discovered she'd unwittingly been filmed while having sex and her sexual partner, a fellow cadet, had broadcast this most private act live via Skype to his buddies. Another woman mustered the courage to speak of an assault by a group of drunken footballers; she remained traumatised years later. What echoed the Hay girls' punishment was this: in every scenario the woman was vilified. The army cadet was disciplined by the army for speaking to outsiders, then dubbed 'that Skype slut' by her peers. The department store publicist was excoriated in the media as a gold-digger betraying the sisterhood with her outsized bid for compensation. When the footballers could deny no more, they tearfully apologised—to their wives, families and employers. In all cases, the mistreated women were cast as liars, sluts, homewreckers. There were slaps on wrists and crocodile tears from the men before they returned to their marriages or moved on to better jobs. The men go on; the women vanish from the story.

This bolt of understanding that contemporary attitudes echoed historical ones, that this loop of hatred seemed ever-repeating, lit a fuse of fury deep inside my writer's brain. But a novel requires years of immersion in your material. This was ugly stuff, bleak and paralysing. Also, where was the complexity in this blunt, stupid hatred? What was there to explore? I couldn't live inside it for the duration of a whole novel. I was no activist, nor commentator, nor polemicist. I certainly didn't see myself as a political writer. How could an artist like me work with material of this kind? How could I respond?

The painter Jasper Johns once said art is what happens when you take an object and do something to it—*and then do something else to it*. It was this 'something else' that slowly emerged, through trial and error, allowing me to stay with the story.

I suspect there may be a relationship between Johns's 'something else' and what the revered acting teacher Uta Hagen called one's 'inner objects'. I've only recently come to Hagen's classic *Respect for Acting*, but am finding it revelatory about the writing process. Among other lessons, Hagen taught the use of 'personal and private objects' with which an actor can enliven their work: 'I refer to such intangibles as colors, textures, music, elements of nature. I must admit that I do not know how to teach this, and I assiduously avoid teaching it. I can only make you aware that these "essences" can be valuable sources ...'

She speaks also of 'release objects':

> . . . a polka dot tie, an ivy leaf on a stucco wall, a smell or
> sound . . . a grease spot on the upholstery, things as seemingly
> illogical as those. I used these small objects as stimuli successfully
> and questioned their logic only in discussion. Later, I learned
> from [a psychiatrist] that this little indirect object was the release
> object, a release of the censor which moves along with us and
> says, 'Don't lose control.'

At the time I was struggling with my book the most, I interviewed
the novelist Amanda Lohrey, who spoke of her need for fiction to
carry some resonance, some hovering meaning beyond that offered
by banal reality.

'There is the literal surface of life,' she told me, 'and then there's
that oceanic meaning underneath . . . [A]ny narrative that doesn't have
a few messages from that realm is, for me, deficient. Too mastered,
too known, too literal.'

For the first time, I saw that a major part of the problem with my
failing novel was fear of my material's darkness, and my overwhelming
desire to control it with constrictive rational thought. And so, I let go.
I changed the time frame from the past to a surreal kind of present,
or a maybe-future. Inner objects and otherworldly messages suddenly
gathered force in my work, releasing my story about a cruel outback

prison for modern young women from the desolate realism I was wrestling with, opening up new narrative possibilities: dreamier, stranger, more metaphorical; darker but more beautiful.

The question of how these objects and messages arose is one I can hardly answer, except to say that once I decided to surrender, once I accepted this book must be written in an almost blind, dreamlike state—that I must not question the driving *illogic* of my subconscious, primitive mind—it began to throw up images and objects that had their own power and which I instinctively understood could make the story grow and move.

What were these things? Often they were natural creatures— a little brown trout, rabbits, kangaroos, cicadas, birds, a frog. But also darker emblems of femininity gone feral: a grotesque doll made from sticks and hair and rabbit skin; shaven heads and cooking pots and ovens and sanitary pads. The objects were mushrooms gathered for poison and a ghostly white horse without its armour-clad knight. They were long dresses grimy with dirt, padlocked leashes conjuring chastity belts, bonnets evoking both blinkers and scold's bridle. They were mad and creepy, and they set my book free.

These objects and messages came from my immediate surroundings, from the media, from dreams, from our collective unconscious, from our history and contemporary culture. Drawn up from the dark, they liberated my novel from the bleak facts of its origin story, and allowed it to move not only narratively—in plot terms—but psychologically. They allowed the characters to form themselves into powerful, flawed individuals, in turn permitting what I hoped was a richer exploration of femaleness and power, of choice and complicity.

§

Let me take you back to that vile graffiti on the fence. For me, the deadening power of that slogan comes not only from my revulsion, or its hatred of all women, but more importantly from the protective impulse triggered in me immediately following that first shock: the impulse to turn away, to ignore—and thereby on some deep and dangerous level to accept and legitimise. The fact that nobody cleaned the words off immediately, that they remained on that fence even for 24 hours, shows that this response had already taken place in other viewers. The hatred worked: anyone who saw that violent, degrading instruction and turned away—who perhaps is seeing it and turning away even now, as I write—has understood and internalised the reality it seeks to create. In turning away, we agree to accept that this message is part of the tolerable, even familiar, fabric of our lives. It is the natural way of things.

But art can give us a way to refuse.

Take an object. Do something to it. Do something else to it. Art can take something as dark as the Hay Institution for Girls, as hateful as that graffiti, and in applying the transfiguring power of 'something else', it can give us the strength not to turn away and normalise, but to *keep looking*—and in doing so to question, provoke, understand, reject, change. The 'something else' of art can turn inner deadness into smouldering embers. If we fan them, they can become fuel and fire, igniting our courage and hope, giving us the power to resist, to speak, transform.

6

Strange Bedfellows

•———————•

The Lady, the unicorn and
The Natural Way of Things

I first saw the medieval *Lady and the Unicorn* tapestries on a visit
to the Musée de Cluny in Paris in 2014. Of course I had seen
scraps of the images before, as we all surely have on a greeting card
or a tea towel; they're such iconic images it's hard to escape them.
But having zero interest in either unicorns or 'ladies', I'd never given
them a second glance.

So when I entered the small dark room in the Cluny where the
tapestries hung, I was utterly unprepared for what happened to me.

The first shock was the quite radical contrast of this room to
every other room we'd seen in the museum. This could be selective
memory, but it seemed that until we reached the tapestries at the

top of the gallery, everything else I'd seen was either military or religious in theme. There were many very beautiful objects, but they all belonged to the world so familiar in museum displays we don't even notice it. What I mean is a supremely male historical world, in which women are either entirely absent or occupy only the most peripheral, functional, one-dimensional roles.

Imagine my surprise, then, on entering this dark room to find an illuminated, brilliantly coloured space entirely dominated by a woman's presence: her body, her desires, her central place in relationship to the world around her. I was at once mesmerised and oddly unnerved.

I stayed in that room for a long time, while other people came and went. The tapestries seemed to hover in the darkness—as, indeed, the occupants of each tapestry appear to hover on their small dark islands within the borders of each one—and I felt that *I* was somehow suspended inside someone else's dream.

The tapestries were created around 1500 in France, commissioned by a member of the Le Viste family. Not much is known about their early years, until they were rediscovered in the nineteenth century in the Château de Boussac, a small castle in Creuse, in central France. They were in quite serious disrepair, damaged by rats and other vandals, but they were acquired and restored by the Musée de Cluny in Paris in 1882, where they have remained ever since.

In 2018 the tapestries travelled to Sydney for exhibition at the Art Gallery of New South Wales. I was lucky enough to see them again, and to be invited to speak about their connection to my novel *The Natural Way of Things*. It was only the third time in 500 years that the tapestries had left France.

There are six large tapestries, each featuring a woman at the centre, surrounded by flowers, trees and many tiny animals, and flanked by a lion and a unicorn. In some, but not all, she is accompanied by a seemingly younger woman, presumably a maidservant. Each of the first five hangings depict one of the five senses: touch, taste, smell, hearing and sight. And then there is a sixth, on which some words appear—*À mon seul désir*, or 'To my sole desire'. And this is the tapestry about which there is most speculation and mystery.

What was it about these images that spoke to me so powerfully that day in Paris?

As I've suggested, the visual language of princesses and flowing dresses and fluffy bunnies and unicorns is one I've deliberately and forcefully rejected throughout my life. The overtly feminine has never felt like my domain. And yet I remained transfixed, because the more I looked the more I found, and it quickly became clear that adorable unicorns and princess gowns were not what was interesting about these pictures. I didn't know then how much they would come to mean to me, but obeying some cloudy instinct, I jotted a few lines about them into my notebook.

I obeyed this instinct despite my confusion because I'm actually no stranger to the feeling of discomfort and compulsion together, for it's a potent mix that often ends up generating raw material for fiction. So I was not surprised when, later, a momentary reference to the tapestries turned up in my novel, a book most often described as a feminist dystopia, about a group of young women held prisoner in the Australian bush.

The girls in my novel don't know why they're in this place, except that they've each been sexually involved with a powerful man, and the resulting scandals have seen them abducted and dumped there, surrounded by a powerful electric fence. After many months, the girls start turning wild and begin roaming the paddocks—Yolanda to trap rabbits for food and Verla searching for mushrooms with which to poison her captors.

One morning Verla thinks back to a trip to Paris with her politician lover. Even after all this time, she's convinced he still cares for her, and that he'll soon arrive to take her home. During their affair he gave her a copy of Walt Whitman's *Leaves of Grass* (just as Bill Clinton did for Monica Lewinsky) and she finds herself recalling it as she roams the landscape.

The song of me rising from bed and meeting the sun. In the soft dewy morning Verla wanders, whispering Whitman. It surprises her, how much she remembers of the book—the lines rustling from her lips as she walks, searching out mushrooms. She knows by heart, of course, those early words he had murmured, nuzzling, when she thought she would burst like fruit from the heaviness of all that fermenting desire.

[. . .]

But now, the grass brushing her calves, soaking the hem of her tunic, and the sun softly warming the earth, it is not plunging tongues and stript chests (but oh, the sweet open planes of his chest, she could cry for it, and did) but other, surprising fragments, things she had not known she knows, that come to her. *And mossy scabs of the wormfence, and heaped stones, and elder and mullen and pokeweed.*

She sees, in the little well between tussocks, a swell of fresh white humps, moves to it. *Alone far in the wilds and mountains I hunt.*

Bending, she grasps the root end of the largest mushroom and lifts it to her face. It smells of earth and dankness, almost human. She runs her fingertips over the soft frills beneath its hood. It's not the one she wants, probably. But still. She drops it with the other, smaller ones into the pockety gloom of the tea-towel sack.

The white of the mushroom cap is the same dusky, chalky white of the horse she had seen in the night. And of the unicorn, in Paris.

In the Musée de Cluny they stood before the tapestries, his thumb stroking hard, desirous, over the bones at the base of her neck. She leaned back into that rhythmic stroking, feasting her own mind and senses on the wondrousness of the tapestry. Shocked at the effect of these hangings on her when all the other old dead things he showed her only bored her, or confused. But here, the reds and bronzes, the small playful rabbits, and the monkey burying its little face in flowers. The virgin holding fast to that unicorn shaft, Verla knew what that felt like in her hand (she was never a virgin with him, but he liked pretending) and back at the hotel they turned over and under one another in the streaming sunlight, and the woven threads of the tapestries all merged inside her: the poetry, the tastes, the smells and sounds and visions, the flowers and harp and My Only Desire and the Body Electric, and Verla knew her life had truly begun.

That was long ago now.

In this passage, the remembered tapestries speak to Verla's fantasies of a cultured, feminine empowerment, and sustain her delusion that her superior worldliness will somehow save her. The memory is an escape from the prison's hardship and isolation into the high glamour of a Parisian dream. In short, the tapestries represent the starkest possible contrast to her present reality. Only much later does Verla understand how deeply she has deceived herself about love and power.

The very fleeting appearance of the *Lady and the Unicorn* tapestries in my book illustrates a process that often happens in the making of a novel. There is the writer's almost completely unconscious selection of a seemingly random image that fits, without any detailed awareness of how that image might hold inside it a great deal of compressed meaning. But when I was invited to speak at the Sydney exhibition I was granted an unusual opportunity: the chance to go back to the tapestries, many times, and to open up just what my subconscious mind may have been doing when it instinctively placed them in my book.

I'm painfully aware of how many art historians and other fine minds have skilfully interpreted these works. By contrast, my own imaginative leaps into and out from the tapestries may be naive, or else plain mad. But at the same time I believe that the exchanges and renewals made possible by great works of art are endless, and endlessly private and peculiar to each person who sees them.

For my own odyssey into these six astonishing works, I chose six elements that particularly spoke to me in connection with my novel.

The first is the centrality of the body—specifically, the female body. Many people who've read *The Natural Way of Things* have remarked on what they call its visceral nature. Some women told me they read the experiences of the girls not with their minds, in the way they usually understand books, but that in some deep, recognising way they read the novel with their bodies. This didn't surprise me, because in a strange way I feel that I *wrote* it with my body.

As I've said, my first big shock at seeing the tapestries in Paris was their entirely sensual and secular nature. In all of them—even the mysterious sixth, which seems to reach for something beyond the physical world—the female body is central. I understand that the sense of touch came first in the medieval hierarchy of the five senses, and it does seem the strongest at work here. The weavings are astonishingly convincing, for example, in rendering texture: we know just by looking whether the women's dresses are made of velvet or of brocade, and I'm sure I'm not alone in having an almost irresistible urge to reach out and touch the fabric to verify what my eye has told me.

Physical sensation is at the heart of every one of these images. On my first viewing I thought how unusually liberated this was, the depiction of a woman delighting in the pleasures of her own senses, without a man or god in sight. But on a second look I saw I was wrong, for the expression of the Lady's senses seems almost always in service to someone or something other than herself. In the 'taste' tapestry, for example, I first saw her reaching for a little sweet to eat—but now it appears she's to feed it to the parrot in her other hand. In 'hearing', she's not only listening to music but playing it, offering it for someone else to enjoy. In 'sight', she doesn't look at herself in the mirror but shows the unicorn *his* image. In 'smell', she may be threading scented flowers for a circlet—but is this for herself or someone else? In the 'touch' tapestry, she steadies the flagpole in one hand while her other clasps the unicorn's horn. It is difficult for a modern viewer to ignore the sexual symbolism here, and in my novel Verla makes that explicit. So in the end I was left to wonder: whose pleasure is important here, in the Lady's sensory adventures? Perhaps, despite her luxurious surroundings, it is still too transgressive for a woman to freely enjoy the delights of her own body.

The second element that spoke to me is the natural world in which the scenes take place—specifically, the garden. The sense of feminine serenity and tranquillity that greets one on first sight of the tapestries is largely created by the profusion of these superbly delicate floral images—the *millefleurs* or thousand flowers—that crowd the background of all the scenes. At first glance the flowers appeared to me almost like stars; there are so many, so thickly scattered, as if the Lady and her animal companions are floating in a shimmering galaxy of flowers. It lends the scenes an otherworldly quality, even while they are anchored in the familiar by the large and recognisable pine, holly, oak and orange trees.

In the catalogue for the exhibition there was a list recording the image and name of every plant in the tapestries. There's blue columbine, yellow foxglove, white swallow-wort and daffodil; there's wild leopard's-bane and birthwort, hyacinth and dog's tooth. I hope my recitation here provides an echo of the Whitman lines in the extract I quoted. That echo has allowed me to see that the repetition of the floral emblems produces a kind of visual hypnosis, mirroring the aural hypnosis of the Whitman poetry as it worked on me when I read it.

In *The Natural Way of Things*, my women are cast into a barren landscape because of their sins of the body. Here, too, I find it impossible to think of a woman in a garden without turning to the myth of the first woman in the first garden, Eve in Eden. And once we do that, we must allow that somewhere in all this lush beauty is also an ancient threat: the woman will be tempted, but she must resist. She knows that if she succumbs to all this pleasure, her fate is sealed.

This brings me to the other half of the natural realm and the third element: the world of animals. Surely this is the most delightful and also the most chaotic aspect of the tapestries, where our various human attitudes towards animals collide. We have the infant sweetness of rabbits and lambs and puppies, the antic playfulness of the small monkey. The lion, usually such a majestic creature, especially in medieval imagery, here often looks like a goofy, distractible younger brother, with his array of theatrical facial expressions, sometimes appealing directly to the viewer as if to say, *Get a load of this!*

The unicorn, I think, is more inscrutable, playing directly to our culture's fairytales and fantasies about girls and horses, and the fetishisation of the virgin state for women. In my novel, Verla is constantly glimpsing a white horse moving through the distant trees, and becomes fixated on the promise of rescue in this vision. I have to confess a rather blind stupidity in this choice, for despite the obviousness of the imagery, the white horse arrived in my novel directly from the real world. When I was working on the book at a friend's farm, the family's elderly white horse, Gidgee, was forever nudging around the edges of my sight, and I could hear her ripping tussocks from the ground and chewing them outside my bedroom at night. Nevertheless, my instinctive use of Gidgee, but none of the *other* horses I saw on the farm, shows how deeply the image of the white horse has embedded itself in the female unconscious, with its connection to womanly passivity and the notion that rescue from captivity can only come from outside ourselves, never from within.

But as with everything in these tapestries, the animal representations are full of contrasts and contradictions. Alongside the soft fur and tiny paws and soulful eyes of the domesticated beasts, there is wildness. The lion occasionally shows his teeth and makes visible his claws; the unicorn's horn is a spike. The cunning fox lurks; or perhaps it's a wolf, ready to attack. Above it all fly the birds with their sharp beaks and talons. The cheetahs and leopards may be hiding among flowers, but they're still predatory, and the gaze the infant unicorn directs at a nearby rabbit in the 'taste' tapestry looks like pure malice, pure threat.

Perhaps the very appeal of these creatures lies in the constant threat of danger, lending a strength and tension to the tapestries which would not be present if all we saw in them were fluffy bunnies and baby lambs.

This sense of menace intensifies in the fourth element I notice, and that is the sense of captivity pervading the whole series. Once more, I think I might have unconsciously detected this sense of restriction or restraint to link the tapestries to what was going on in my novel.

The first, most obvious sign of this is the sharp visual jolt of the heavily chained monkey in the 'touch' tapestry. Elsewhere, the monkey is a mischievous, playful creature with agency and freedom— snatching up a rose to sniff, nibbling on berries or other morsels as it lounges among the flowers—but in this image the monkey is tethered by the neck to a heavy stone, gaunt-faced in stillness and misery.

Once you notice the chained monkey, you begin to see other signs of bondage: many of the animals, especially the wild ones, are collared or have remnants of chains attached. The falcon may fly, but its legs are ringed with cuffs and cords, implying capture at any time. The collars on the dogs and cheetahs may be jewelled, but we all know their real function is not decorative. These ornamented trappings of animal captivity led me, then, to look again at the women's adornments. The gorgeous golden necklaces start to look heavy, and I'm reminded that jewels are also stones; the roped belts take on the look of leashes, the wide bracelets turn to manacles before my eyes. Even the women's hair is tied and roped, and in the sixth tapestry we are left to wonder: is the Lady freeing herself from her jewelled shackles, or putting them on by choice?

The idea of female complicity in our own oppression is something I was keen to explore in my novel, but only now am I reminded of just how much the decorative iconography of womanhood has always involved this mimicry, the chains and ropes of adornment so easily evoking a jailer's equipment.

The fifth angle on these tapestries that interests me is sisterhood, or the relationship between women, and its complications. In four of the six tapestries, the Lady is accompanied, or attended, by another young woman. Most often seen as a maidservant or lady-in-waiting, the second woman is smaller in stature, presumably younger, and fairly obviously less powerful than the Lady. I'm intrigued by the two women's facial expressions in these images. In contemporary depictions of relationships between women there's an epidemic of ecstatic smiling—indeed, women are now constantly exhorted to *smile more* by colleagues, friends or even strangers in the street. It's true that in several of the tapestries there's the possibility of a smile emerging on the face of the Lady, but it often looks to me more like distraction than pleasure, and the servant girl usually appears either downcast or bored out of her skull.

I suppose I'm focusing on this aspect of the tapestries to gently note that even in scenes of supposedly tranquil luxury and ease, relationships between people—and between women—are rarely unaffected by power. One of the things that bothered many readers of my novel is that my captive young women frequently don't like each other, nor do they pragmatically band together for mutual benefit. It seemed to me self-evident that a shared crisis doesn't necessarily result in unity between individuals—even if it would be in everyone's best interests—so this level of unease among readers surprised me.

It also reminded me of how prevalent is our desire to cast women as saintly or noble or sweet, when the truth is that a woman can be just as competitive and protective of her power as any man. The Lady at the centre of the tapestries may look benevolent, but her status in relation to the only other human figure in these scenes is clear. She holds power over the younger woman, and she won't be relinquishing it any time soon.

The last aspect of the tapestries that intrigues me is the often-discussed element of mystery that surrounds them. There are the unknown details of their origins, of course, but more interesting to me is the sense of the uncanny that arises from the images themselves.

As I wrote *The Natural Way of Things*, I was conscious of needing a presence, or a perception of meaning, that came from beyond the known, literal world around us. This was something I'd created in my own peculiar first novel, *Pieces of a Girl*, and then largely abandoned, but I came to realise that the strange and difficult story I was trying to tell now could perhaps only work if I opened myself up to the spectral, the menacing, the dream.

I think now that it's this hallucinatory feeling that compelled me to sit with the tapestries for so long in the Cluny that day. And the more I look at them now, the more they overflow with strangeness and disorientating contradiction.

This arises at least partly from their spatial composition. Dogs and monkeys and rabbits often float in the air above the Lady along with the birds—or are they, rather, *behind* her, in an endlessly deep visual field of flowers? Most of the flowers themselves do not grow from any earth but blossom effortlessly in air. There are other striking contradictions: a breeze flutters one banner but not its twin; the animals' faces are immensely expressive while the women's remain impassive; and the scale of the creatures seems to shrink and swell at random—a monkey is here tinier than a rabbit, there larger than a cow. The most exotic creatures can appear to be tame while domesticated beasts run wild.

The centre of the mystery, though, is surely the unicorn itself, that mythical creature of Bible and legend, shifting and transforming between childhood innocence and adult carnality, bringing with it always the ephemeral yearnings of fantasy and dream.

As I said earlier, a state of not knowing, a feeling of intense confusion, is often what sends me to the page to wrestle with it in the form of fiction. But this uncertainty can be very frightening when you are midway through the long process of resolving a work of art. To free myself from the sometimes-paralysing fear of uncertainty, I've learned a few mental tricks. One of these is to conceive of my story in progress as a kind of performance that I am only there to witness, rather than control. And in my mind's eye, the unfolding performance of my novel has always taken place in the hushed dark of a richly textured circus tent—one that looks very like the tent of the sixth tapestry, which might enclose the Lady once the lion and the unicorn let fall its drapes.

Of course this tiny coincidence is meaningless to anyone else, but to me, the blue and gold tent feels like an encouraging omen, an accidental gift passed through the centuries from one unknown artist to another.

I believe that the greatest works of art do speak to us in this very private way, and that the quiet space between maker and viewer—between writer and reader—is where the most profound transformations of art can take place. It's in this space that each of us, if we are entranced, can claim the work for ourselves and make it new.

7

Letting in the Light

• ——————— •

Sharing unfinished work: risks and joys

In Virginia Woolf's *To the Lighthouse*, amateur artist Lily Briscoe
stands on the edge of the lawn at the Ramsays' house, brushes
in hand, concentrating on her painting at the easel. Lily, a guest, is
working on a loose, modernist picture of Mrs Ramsay and her child
sitting in the window. But 'even while she looked at the mass, the
line, the colour', Lily is distracted by her own wariness, her fear that
someone will come and look at her picture while she's making it.
Soon, another guest appears beside her to do just that; Lily is appalled.
And yet, because it is the perceptive Mr Bankes and not one of the
others (whose inspections she 'could not have endured'), mingled
with her distress is something else:

She would have snatched the picture off the easel, but she said to herself, One must. She braced herself to stand the awful trial of someone looking at her picture. One must, she said, one must. And if it must be seen, Mr Bankes was less alarming than another. But that any other eyes should see the residue of her thirty-three years, the deposit of each day's living, mixed with something more secret than she had ever spoken or shown in the course of all those days was an agony. At the same time it was immensely exciting.

At the same time it was immensely exciting. I wonder if other artists reading this novel have reacted as viscerally as I do to this paragraph, and the truth of its last sentence? For it speaks to a paradox at the heart of the artist's work: the need for absolute privacy and the fear of exposure, while knowing at the same time that soon this exposure is the very thing we most want and need.

It's true, I believe, that the most reliable satisfactions of the creative life come during the process of making. A writer friend tells me that once a book of his goes to print, the fun part of writing a novel is over. Then comes publication, 'all the un-fun part', he says. 'It's all downhill from there.'

I'd say most of us recognise this feeling to some degree. And yet it's also true that we would not keep writing books if we knew nobody would read them. The reader isn't just a passive recipient, after all—they're the other half of the invention. For me, at least, a book without a reader would be like a garden no one's allowed to enter. A garden with no visitor to see its varying shades of green and grey, to hear the scuttle of its tiny lizards, inhale its obscure, particular mix of smells, or run an open hand across its leaves? Better the wilderness.

§

Lily Briscoe's halting progress with her painting is an attempt, working along the nerve, 'struggling against terrific odds to maintain her courage', to bring the vision of her inner world into full expression on canvas in the outer one. But she faces an adversity familiar to all artists. 'She could see it all so clearly, so commandingly, when she looked: it was when she took her brush in hand that the whole thing changed.' Her vision fragments and dissolves in the journey from eye to canvas, and in that moment's faltering she's visited by all the other shortcomings of her life—'her own inadequacy, her insignificance, keeping house for her father off the Brompton Road'—all converging in a confirmation of the dreadful truth: her failure as an artist.

Lily begins her painting at the start of this novel and finishes it from the same position on the lawn at the end, eleven years later, in a devastatingly altered world. In those intervening years she has reached her artistic maturity along with an acceptance of herself and her place in the world. Her vision is no longer fragmented, no longer so full of doubt and self-condemnation. By the last line of the book, she and her talent are now whole.

The tension between the need to work in private and exhibit in public is something that has long preoccupied me. I don't think it's purely to do with whether a work is ready for viewing, for even when one knows the work is complete and we've given it every part of ourselves, trepidation about its exposure can be intense. It's not even really a matter of whether people 'like' the work, though a positive reception surely helps. I think the tension is a deeper one, more likely caused by a collision of the private and public selves: the introversion and psychic nakedness required to do the imaginative work, clashing with the blended self-protection and surrender needed for the artwork's release into the world.

There's another space between those extremes of private creation and public exposure, though, and it's an area I'm curious about. This is a kind of holding space, somewhere we might bring an *unfinished* work to be exposed to the scrutiny of others. I'm interested in the need many of us have to share a work in order to be able to complete it.

What's going on when one artist asks another to look at a work in progress? What are we asking for? And on the other side of the exchange, as the respondent, how might we best proceed?

§

Writing is one of a very few art forms we think of as a completely solitary practice. Visual artists often share studios and other resources, and performance is by necessity collaborative. Musicians rarely work entirely alone, and filmmaking is a wholly communal experience. Perhaps musical composition comes closest in its solitariness. But fiction writing in particular is produced by introversion and isolation. Perhaps that's why there are so many books about it; maybe, like this one, they're an attempt to find the conversation and community that's built in to other art forms but lacking in ours.

I once had the privilege of watching the development and early rehearsals of a new stage play in production at a major theatre company in Sydney. It felt transgressively voyeuristic and exciting, watching the emergence of a work of art in real time. This would have been a laughable confession to the director and actors, of course; for them, the idea of privacy in performance would be a contradiction in terms.

At the start of each scene I would watch the director in *her* watching. It was fascinating to see the intensity of her attention and its manifestation in her body. At first she'd rest back in her seat, legs stretched out before her, arms crossed behind her head. As the scene progressed she drew gradually, slowly forwards, and by its end she'd unknowingly curved into an almost full-body crouch. When the scene ended the released tension seemed to catapult her from her seat onto the stage, where she would stride around among the actors, inspecting them and their space from different angles. Then she would speak to each of the actors individually, quietly but not at all in private, squatting with the script pages on the floor between them. They would talk together, brows furrowed, trying to get to the heart of a blurriness or hesitance in what had just taken place. There was talk of searching and finding, hunting down the precise meaning in a word or gesture. A lengthy discussion took place about one actor's line: 'I don't know.' Was this dismissal, puzzlement, fear? Did he mean 'nobody told me', 'I'm confused, but interested', or 'get fucked'? I was astounded at how many possibilities actor and director discovered. How many different moods and implications they found, in this focused attention together on those same three words.

More recently, I sat in on a 'table read' of a play based on one of my novels. The playwright was renowned and experienced, as were the actors whose task was to read aloud the first draft of her play. As the term suggests, we sat around a table, accompanied by the company's artistic director and others, each of us with the script before us, and away the actors went. The playwright, whom I knew to be a highly sensitive person, took pages and pages of notes as they read.

It went smoothly; the draft was an accomplished one and, afterwards, remarks were made about its high quality. But it was still a first draft, and there was work yet to do. The responses began: actors, director and associated production staff making observations and asking questions, digging into and interrogating the text. The playwright nodded, concentrating intently, took more notes and asked the occasional question herself. Mostly, though, she just listened, without defending or explaining. Everyone in the room was not just accustomed to this process but expert at it. They were entirely respectful, while thorough in their examination of every aspect of the script as it had been read aloud.

I sat transfixed, stunned by the playwright's courage. To open up a first draft in this way, to hand it over to strangers to be pulled apart and wrestled with at such a delicate early stage; to be forced to hear one's infelicities or missteps spoken out loud, *in front of others*! This was my idea of writer's hell.

I came away from the session still impressed, but rigid with tension. The playwright wasn't. She came away with a head full of ideas and excitement about the next draft. And I saw how this early opening up, this true collaboration, was an essential step in a play's development. It was already allowing the work to change and breathe, moving closer even now to the fulfilment of its own vision.

Theatre is a truly communal enterprise, of course. But do other, less obviously collaborative artists also gain from exchanges about their work as it's being made?

Painters, for example, often seem to welcome 'intrusion' into their studios, and I've always been surprised by how willing they are to share work in progress with onlookers. Perhaps it's born of situations like Lily Briscoe's, painting *en plein air*, the work emerging in full view of any passer-by. Or maybe it comes from their training in shared classrooms or studios, working naturally and openly alongside one another. Writers might learn in class with others too, but we can't inspect each other's first stumbling attempts by merely glancing across the room. Any sharing is a highly self-conscious, invitation-only affair.

Some visual artists, like the renowned painter Jude Rae, actually prefer their work in progress to be exposed to another gaze at some point. For Rae, this gaze doesn't even need to result in an opinion. The viewer—who could be anybody, she says, not necessarily someone with art expertise—need not speak, nor offer any non-verbal cues, in order for Rae to benefit from the mere fact of their looking. This has nothing to do with seeking approval, and everything to do with her own separation from the work. 'It pushes me away from the painting,' she says, 'and somehow enhances the objectivity I can bring to it.'

Sometimes she'll consider what the observer has to say, if anything, but for the painter the beneficial alchemy of this 'exchange' is almost totally internal. It leads to a 'useful alienation' of artist from picture. 'When someone else looks at my work I see it with the eyes of a stranger. It's not always a comfortable process.'

§

Writers have to enjoy solitude for the most part; it's a job condition. But eventually, we must let others into the making of a book. For many of us, these others come to the work only at the end of its creation, as our literary agents or editors and publishers. But some writers find it essential to share a decidedly *un*finished or early draft work with trusted intimates much earlier in the process.

For many years I've been sustained and creatively enriched by conversation with a small gaggle of writer friends. Our talk is for purposes of encouragement, consolation or entertainment; there's a lot of bitter laughter, for example, about the more humiliating public aspects of a writer's life. But these exchanges also have a questing, challenging quality. They prod me to question myself more deeply, and to work harder. After some years of solitary work, and often when blocked by some intransigence in the manuscript, I realise with a combination of exhaustion and hopelessness that I need to 'get it away from me'. This means handing over a draft of my developing book for one or other of these writer friends to read. And then we talk about it.

The sharing of work in progress can be a highly risky exercise. It must be done at the right time, and with the right reader. Power relationships are dangerous here: a strong opinion delivered too early can send the writer down misleading tracks, and all artists have surely experienced the destruction that can be wrought by blunt criticism from the wrong person at a delicate early stage. This is why I've always been wary of the kind of workshopping that takes place in creative writing classes. As a student myself, too many times I watched a talented beginner sitting in a state of unbearable shame as a clumsy classmate tore apart a story's embryonic tissue. The risk here is not just embarrassment but real harm to a writer's ability or willingness to grow and experiment, to risk, to reach beyond what they know they can do. And when such criticism comes from someone with no expertise themselves, what is there to learn? Beginners can be savagely opinionated critics (all artists must beware the person who eagerly offers feedback with a promise to be 'brutally honest'), and classrooms are full of dimly understood agendas and competitive urges. Even a careful teacher can't always protect a student from these, and sometimes the damage is permanent.

This kind of blundering criticism is one risk of sharing too early—but constant support and affirmation can present a different kind of problem. If someone is encouraging about a certain aspect of a work in progress, newer writers in particular, yet to develop strong artistic instincts, are at risk of wandering away from their own obscure and difficult (but true) path to go sniffing after the scent of that early reader's praise.

In the early years of writing, it's natural to want encouragement. But the premature and frequent sharing of work in progress can hinder development of the self-reliance every artist needs. The approval or otherwise gained by sharing work at every stage of development, as can happen in writing groups and classes, in online fora or on social media, can fuel a neurotic addiction to external validation, reassurance or correction. It can create blankness in the self, an inability to discern the worth of one's own work even at a sentence level without outside help. And it means we can fail to develop and exercise the artist's most important muscles: fortitude, astute self-critique and perseverance— even bloody-mindedness when necessary—in our commitment to our art. F. Scott Fitzgerald is supposed to have said that 'all good writing is swimming underwater, holding your breath'. We have to get used to holding that breath for a long, long time.

And yet. With my own work in progress there always comes a time when I need a fellow writer's eyes upon it. For me that point is usually around three-quarters of the way towards a book's completion, when it's sturdy enough to withstand a good critical nudge without collapse, yet still malleable enough to allow substantial change.

Some writers see this need for another's involvement as a sign of amateurism, a failure of nerve or skill. (Even as I write this, I feel the faint surge of nausea that comes with self-exposure. Like Lily Briscoe, haunted by the recurring echo of Mr Tansley's sneers: 'Women can't paint, women can't write . . .') But to be honest, I see it as the opposite of timidity. It takes guts to ask for a deep reading of and critical response to unfinished work, especially if one then decides to reject that response entirely. Even if the only outcome is a strengthening of my own resolve, it always yields improvement of some kind.

For a start, there's what Jude Rae describes as 'useful alien-ation'. When Rae described how her onlooker's response could be both irrelevant and essential, I realised there was a parallel in the writing life. As I've said, often it's an insoluble problem that has prompted me to send my lumpy draft to a colleague. But quite often, as soon as I've sent it the solution I've been seeking has suddenly revealed itself. In the olden days before email, this sometimes happened literally at the moment I heard the envelope thump onto the postbox floor.

This echoes Rae's experience, I think. There's a dropping away of attachment, a necessary disenchantment and an acceptance that something really is wrong, rather than continuing to haul the thing along with hope, wishing it were otherwise. And in that surrender, the mind stops grasping and relaxes, allowing potential solutions to arise unbidden.

But for me this detachment is just the start of the process. Occasionally I'll ask my colleague reader to focus on a particular aspect of the manuscript, but these days what's most important is the nature of the conversation that happens after the reading. There's trepidation, but also a new feeling of lightness, as if the project has been somehow oxygenated, and there's a surge of new possibility and energy. It's as if all the doors and windows of my house are flung open and fresh air and sunlight are streaming in.

But how does this actually happen? What does the colleague reader *do* to allow me to see this new potential? Sometimes it's a matter of their identifying a falsity of voice I hadn't noticed. Or urging me to venture further into an area I'd been unconsciously avoiding. Sometimes there's a knot of logic I haven't been able to untie, but they show me the end of the thread so I can pick it up and begin the untangling. Sometimes they've pointed to an aspect of the book and asked, 'Why?' And sometimes they simply say, keep going, you're almost home.

I'm fortunate that my colleague readers have an ideal temperament for this kind of conversation, which is curious rather than emphatic or directive. This temperament depends on a few qualities, starting with generosity—and that includes being willing to praise.

I've heard it said that writers live on praise. It feels a little shaming to admit this, but I think it's true. All the colleague readers I've worked with understand, as I do in looking at their work, that praise at this unfinished stage is not about ego-stroking or flattery, but about energy and ideas. Virginia Woolf put it this way, writing in her diary about the public reception of *To the Lighthouse*: 'What is the use of saying one is indifferent . . . when positive praise, though mingled with blame, gives one such a start on, that instead of feeling dried up one feels, on the contrary, flooded with ideas?'

This is the point: the right kind of praise draws an artist out of fugitive self-defence and into a sense of abundance and willingness to risk. Another point is that, because the artist is exposing work when it is still full of flaws, out of balance, ungainly in a hundred ways, any praise provides only the smallest counterweight to their own savage fear and self-criticism.

It might sound ridiculous to some people, but the anxiety involved in creativity can be extreme. Here's Lily Briscoe again: 'It was in that moment's flight between the picture and her canvas that the demons set on her who often brought her to the verge of tears and made this passage from conception to work as dreadful as any walk down a dark passage for a child.'

I don't know why this should be so, only that it is. But a psychologist friend once explained to me that, in evolutionary terms, the human sense of safety depends on the certainty of belonging to one's tribe. Being alone represents a profound danger; separation or rejection has, at its heart, a fear of annihilation and death. But good art comes from the risk-taking act of departure from the group, from striking out alone, away from accepted codes and norms. So when we make a choice to reveal to others just how far we have ventured from the tribe, when we stand there alone, holding out our imaginations for inspection, it makes sense that the old primal response is to perceive this vulnerability as almost life-threatening, even while the conscious mind knows that's absurd.

But the generosity in this exchange isn't just about the reader praising the writer; it goes both ways. The writer must genuinely allow the invited reader their response, however challenging or mistaken it might feel. And they must listen to it—*really* listen—without defensiveness or qualification, just as the playwright did at the table read that day. This the same generosity embedded in any exchange of gifts. It's not just the giver who gets to be generous; the gracious acceptance of the gift is an act of generosity in return.

Even if everything in the writer wants to reject the early reader's response, we must pay attention, for this speaks to an important truth about making art. Once you've sent it into the world it doesn't belong to you anymore, and its audience has as much right to its interpretation as you do to your intention. Giving up trying to control what people think of you(r work) is a mark of adulthood, after all.

Humility is another essential part of these conversations, on both sides. I don't mean just modesty, but a willingness to bow down to the work, surrender to it, serve it and not our egos. We need humility to accept that our work reveals things about us that we may not like, but if they are true, we must let them stand.

For Lily Briscoe, the artist's humility lies in facing the truth of the painter she is rather than the one she might wish to be. The spectre of Mr Paunceforte, the successful ('real') painter admired by all, is ever-present in Lily's mind when she looks at her work, comparing.

She could have wept. It was bad, it was bad, it was infinitely bad! She could have done it differently of course; the colour could have been thinned and faded; the shapes etherealised; that was how Paunceforte would have seen it. But she did not see it like that.

She did not see it like that. I think all artists must at some stage face this forlorn discovery: I am not like others, and all I have to offer are my own perceptions. You can try to hide, to impress, but I believe good art only comes from the imperfect true self, first accepted and then revealed.

On the part of the colleague reader, I think humility is to do with this same surrender, attending to the potential of *this* book, here, now—not a previous book, or a different one, the one I myself might write, but this one. It's to do with gentleness, as well: not leaping too quickly to 'helpful' judgements or quick, dramatic solutions. It might mean waiting, admitting that I don't know what's required, but I sensed something hidden, or an instability of logic, or a tonal incongruity I can't quite put my finger on. It means forgoing any expert status, accepting that there's much we still don't know about this work, but that hopefully by circling it together, we might uncover its path to completion.

I said earlier that power-based relationships are dangerous in this kind of exchange—and even well-meaning teachers and mentors need to be especially careful. Any suggestion of the invited reader's desire to control, any certainty that an offered solution is the only or best one, should ring warning bells. Humility means a real attentiveness to the promise that is perhaps still lying some way beneath the surface, to be uncovered only if we sit quietly enough, listening hard.

And sitting quietly is difficult. When we writers talk about revising, the big stuff is often what takes our attention. Slashing thousands of words, cutting out characters, shifting chapters, hiving off endings or switching points of view can be exhilarating. Yet what's often forgotten, by writers most of all, is how a manuscript can be changed by painstaking work at the level of the sentence, the word.

One of my instructions to myself towards the end of a book is to move through it carefully, 'taking out the lies'. This is a form of tinkering that can radically alter the feeling and authority of a book. In this context, a 'lie' might be a cliché or a moment of pretentiousness, a false note, a sentence that sounds impressive but which I don't really understand or believe. It's fine needlework, exacting and slow, weighing the rhythm and balance of sentences, word by word by word. And it can transform a book.

While 'humility' might evoke smallness, its effect can be profound, allowing the work to fully reveal itself rather than having the writer try to overpower it. It can create the necessary sense that the artwork before us remains open and dynamic, that the potential for new revelation stays alive, vibrant right up until the very last moment of completion.

Generosity and humility combine, I think, in courage—another essential aspect of conversation about unfinished work. The invited reader must have the courage to tell the truth about what they see, even when it might cause pain, even if they're unsure about whether they're right. And the writer needs the courage to hear and accept things they don't want to hear. Usually, what I do not want to hear is: *There is a great deal more work to do.* An even greater form of courage is also required, though: the bravery to reject the advice if necessary, and strike out even further from your tribe. It's quite often easier to take advice than stick with your instincts, but every artist has to learn the difference between reasonable adjustment and fatal capitulation.

§

At the end of *To the Lighthouse*, Lily Briscoe's painting is finally resolved.

> With a sudden intensity, as if she saw it clear for a second, she
> drew a line there, in the centre. It was done; it was finished. Yes,
> she thought, laying down her brush in extreme fatigue, I have
> had my vision.

That final declarative mark is the one Lily has always known is needed, and yet only in that final moment can she see how to make it.

Any artist, one hopes, is always groping forward to new insights, to that discovery just beyond our field of vision. With each new work, we learn essential things, and are sometimes elated by the revelatory nature of those lessons. And yet almost instantly, each time, I find the lesson sinks away, to be absorbed and replaced by the lost feeling that returns as I find, yet again, that I do not know how to write *this* book. It's only by trudging out into that unknown space and starting work, often in the wrong place, wandering down many false tracks, getting lost and finding my way again too many times, that I'll slowly find out.

My colleague readers and I have a running joke that none of us is allowed to die until all our books have been written. We need each other, not only for company or moral support or to fix a problem in a book, but because those trusting, reaching conversations are so exhilarating, so rich. They open up the writer's mind for the definitive pattern to reveal itself at last, allowing each of us to find and mark that precious resolving line and with it bring the vision, finally and fully, into coherence.

8

Cat and Baby

•————————•

On intuition vs pragmatism

A small stray cat approaches two houses on a rainy night. It makes to slip into the first, but is frightened by a sturdy baby clomping down a dimly lit hallway towards it. The cat appears at the next house, where I've been waiting. I silently open the door and flatten myself against the wall, willing it to come inside. I meet its eyes as it crouches, reluctant, shivering in the rain. A few large, rotting frangipani leaves fall in spears to the path, and the creature decides. It darts through the falling wet leaves, past me into the dark house.

On waking I know this for certain as a dream about writing. The cat is my work, and everything else in the dream is me: both houses, the clumsy baby scaring the cat away, the quietly opening door through which the wary creature enters at last.

The images speak to the uncomfortable tension I've long felt between two opposing forces in my creative self. There's the dreamer; the mystery seeker, the watcher for spooky symbols and signals from other realms. This is the self who finds surprises, neither biddable nor controllable, blossoming up from the deep unconscious. Then there's the pragmatist who trusts in hard work and grit, discipline and routine, who's irked by tortured-artist dramatics, and who brings a novel into life as much through determination and tenacity—sometimes even resentment—as any more inspired impulse. For long periods of a book's development, it's the pragmatist who keeps the thing on the rails.

As detailed in an earlier chapter, some years ago I undertook a formal study of the texture of several writers' creative process, including my own. How does fiction form in the mind, moment to moment? How much of my work is done by the stomping baby, how much by the wild, capricious cat? I was fairly aware of my deliberate techniques, but I wanted to understand whether there might also be other, less conscious methods at work. I wanted to investigate whether there were any methods I used *without knowing* I was using them.

I learned that there were, and that they fell into two broad categories. The first was a series of methods for generating the raw material of a book that involved obscure hunches, blind instinct and almost no logic at all. These methods seemed to come from the subconscious, dreaming mind, and to work best when left unquestioned. I called them: 'heat-seeking'; 'drilling, digging and diving'; 'connecting and merging'; and 'waiting or suspending'. The second category was governed by more conscious thought, and applied more diagnostically. These methods worked as problem solvers, applicable only once I had some material on the page to handle. I called them: 'circling and cycling'; 'disrupting or overturning'; 'impersonating or embodying'; 'territory-mapping'; and 'forecasting and hypothesising'.

Other writers will intuitively recognise many of these. Heat-seeking, for example, means following anything that gives the writer even a glimmer of energy. It might be something as tiny as an image or a word, or as conceptually broad as war, or death. The only criterion for 'heat' is that the writer is energised by the thought of it, and that writing 'into' it fuels more writing. Learning to trust your instinct for 'heat', especially when lacking any rational reason to do so, seems to me an important step in every artist's development.

Connecting and merging unalike concepts or things is a well-documented hallmark of creative thought. Digging/diving and circling/cycling are related, though subtly different, and involve returning to existing material to re-examine it, turn it over, try again from a different angle. Annie Dillard's famous quotation of Thoreau gets closest to this one: 'Know your own bone: gnaw at it, bury it, unearth it and gnaw at it still.'

Waiting or suspending—almost a non-process—will also be familiar to many writers. The novelist Joan London once quoted Kipling to me: 'When your Daemon is in charge, do not try to think consciously. Drift, wait, and obey'—which pretty much sums it up, although knowing whether it's your Daemon or your laziness in charge is a trickier question. There's a line between deliberate 'waiting' and nervy avoidance, and only the writer herself can know the difference.

When I recall the writing of my most recent novel, *The Weekend*, a comedy of manners about growing older and friendship between women, one clear source of heat jumps out at me. I'd hoped for an easy ride with this book, unlike the difficult years spent dwelling on the theme of misogyny for my previous novel, *The Natural Way of Things*. With *The Weekend* I wanted to write an antidote, something joyful. I wanted to rest in it, amusing myself with an acerbic portrayal of ordinary friendship between women (albeit a tense and scratchy friendship; I need more than a few drops of acid to stay interested, for 'niceness' turns out to be a creative dead end for me). I envisaged a wry celebration of domestic realism, without the frightened wading through my unconscious that the previous book had demanded.

But soon a decrepit, geriatric dog arrived in my 'joyful' story and began giving off uncanny vibes. It seemed my writing mind wasn't ready to abandon the surrealism that had suffused my girls-in-a-desert-prison book, and *The Weekend*'s Finn, a dementing, staggering labradoodle, emerged as a carrier of abstruse, unnerving messages. For a long time, I had no idea why the ghostly aspect of Finn was important, and the insolubility of this question made me anxious. But I knew enough to trust the heat when I felt it.

That long time became a new lesson for me in 'waiting or suspending': a complete abandonment of all writing for several months. At that point in the process I had three fractious friends trapped in a house together by the sea at Christmas, but no idea why or what was keeping them there. Perseverance wasn't helping me, and nor was anything else. There was no engine for the story. I'd received a prestigious fellowship to write the novel and I dreaded failing my benefactors, but forcing and pushing the writing along—relying purely on my long-cherished work ethic—was simply not working. It was time to stop.

In twenty-five years of writing I'd never abandoned ship like this. There would be no note-taking, no sneaky observing or musing, no attention at all devoted to the world of the book. It felt like giving up, and I was afraid, but by that stage surrender even to that possibility was a relief. For six long months I enjoyed a sedate income-generating and domestic life. I taught, travelled, gardened. I did those household chores neglected when you're absorbed by work: had the leaking roof fixed, cleaned windows, tidied cupboards under sinks. But most artists, I think, will understand the queasy feeling that inevitably comes, the melancholy ache, when you've been away from work too long. I had to go back.

I returned the only way I could, in pure pragmatist mode. I reread, prodded and poked at the stalled book, pushing through resistance for weeks, making no progress. But at some stage a tiny hairline fracture in the problem's sealed casing appeared, then widened—and then cracked open. I still remember the part of the bathroom wall I was staring at when the thought arrived, mid-shower: it wasn't just a house, it was *their dead friend Sylvie's house*. They were there to clean it out for sale. The friends are not merely crabby with one another; they're *lost* to one another. Kipling's Daemon had finally come to the rescue, and from there I was on my way. Finn's pathetic ghostliness now made sense—he was sometimes himself, sometimes a mirror, sometimes a mute and fearsome messenger from Sylvie. He reveals to each woman the illusions she's held about herself until now, and the truths she must face in her time left on this earth.

One thing my study showed me is that different books will demand different processes to dominate their creation. While the origins of *The Natural Way of Things* were dreamlike and primitive, the more pragmatic among my nine processes turned out to be most useful in getting it written. Overturning, for example, saw me abandon a setting in the past and a naturalistic prose style, flipping both to result in a near-future setting and a slightly fantastical, surreal narrative style. Impersonation helps bolster a writer's flagging confidence by imaginatively taking on characteristics of another artist, writer—even another art form or thing. As detailed earlier, for *The Natural Way of Things* I clung secretly to visual artist Louise Bourgeois as my psychic guide. In my mind, the mighty Bourgeois would not waste her time hand-wringing in feeble anxiety, worrying endlessly about *why* she was doing it. Her real motives were immaterial—my imaginary artist persona made me braver.

I've suggested that the processes fell naturally into the two categories—unconscious and conscious, or dreamy and pragmatic. The truth is that in practice they're not so easily separable. The membrane between them is porous, their expression interdependent, dynamic and often simultaneous. What I've slowly come to accept is that the tension I've found so uncomfortable throughout my writing life—that space between the two kinds of thinking—is perhaps the defining feature of the artist's vocation. The baby might be clumsy, but it also directs and corrects, guiding the Daemon creature to arrive, at last, in the right place.

The lesson it seems I must learn over and over, probably forever, is that the indistinct space, the gap or overlap or blur, is where creativity actually lives. And however uneasily, we artists must make our homes there too. We need the grit before we can earn and accept the gift of that surprise moment, when the work finally opens up to us and shows us how to make it.

9

An Element of Lightness

———•———

Laughter as a creative force

If you feel as I do, some days you'll see no hope for humanity. We've destroyed much of the natural world already and seem hell-bent on continuing. Even before the COVID-19 pandemic, people all over the planet were suffering unspeakable violence and deprivation, and now it's worse. We, the affluent, are unwilling to share our wealth with those who most need help, and we spend our time and money on pursuits that wreak ever more moral and environmental destruction. At the same time, we in the wealthiest nations suffer ever-rising levels of anxiety and depression.

In the face of all this, I've been thinking about laughter and what it means, about the possibilities it might hold for all of us. It might seem trivial, or nonsensical even, when the world is in such trouble. But we need radical solutions, and I'm idealistic enough to suggest that if we think seriously about the meaning and implications of laughing, it might open up our minds and our hearts, and start to allow some of the reframing we so desperately need.

Another word for idealism might be delusion, I'm well aware. But this is home territory for me and for all artists, whose daily lives depend on the vigorous deployment of rampant delusion. We must constantly believe in something that doesn't exist, believe it's worth pursuing, believe—all evidence to the contrary—that our seed of a kooky idea will bear fruit. All art in the making is delusion, until you're standing in front of *Blue Poles* or watching *Hamlet* or *Mad Max*, or sitting tearful on your couch into the night, speechless at the genius of Hilary Mantel. It's all delusion, until it's not.

So what do I mean when I say *laughter*, as opposed to comedy, or even humour? The distinction is perhaps a fine one, but also to my mind important. What I'm talking about is something beyond, deeper and broader than comedy; a sense of lightness, of joy, a sense of possibility that comes when laughter enters a work of art, whether it's manifest on the page or merely part of the writer's process. For laughter is a sharp instrument, it turns out, capable of performing many crucial, even profound functions.

I was led to consider this because for several years following the publication of my novel *The Natural Way of Things*—and for the three years during which I wrote it—I was thinking and speaking so much about anger. That book concerned our society's punishment of young women for speaking out against sexual mistreatment, and it was first published in 2015, a couple of years before the Me Too movement exploded around the globe. It took a long time to accept my own anger about the degradation of women in all societies. I've not personally been oppressed in any remarkable way, other than the ways all women are, and that is a mark of my privilege and the many forms of pure luck I've had through my life. But on behalf of my gender and because of the inequality women continue to fight—especially those unprotected by Whiteness and wealth—angry I will remain.

I was deep in middle age before I learned that anger could be a productive creative tool. Creative anger, as I think of it now, is the kind of fury that can be channelled and harnessed. It burns slow and low, as fuel for producing art full of charge and fire. But while it can be artistically productive, and even absolutely liberating, when rage is not counterbalanced by other energy sources it is also, in my experience, completely exhausting. If I want to keep working, writing purely from anger will be impossible.

More importantly, though, I've come to realise that laughter—this sense of lightness and playfulness and optimism—might in fact be productive anger's most effective, most influential friend.

Laughter and pain are inextricably linked in life, as anyone who has snorted at a macabre joke at a loved one's deathbed knows.

A friend of mine whose brother died as a small baby tells me that when her father sat the other children down to deliver this horrific news, she and her brother—and her father too—began to laugh. They roared laughing, in fact. And then they cried and cried.

Just before my own father died, when my siblings and I were teenagers, he told us not to feel guilty if we found ourselves laughing about his death. 'Inappropriate' laughter, he so compassionately told us, was a natural impulse of which we must never be ashamed.

A decade later, when my mother was terminally ill at home, one afternoon during months of difficulty and sadness, her house erupted in riotous shrieks. One sibling had playfully flicked another with water, and soon a full-blown water fight was in action. A friend of my mother's arrived half an hour into this to find all five of us pelting around the house, screaming with laughter, panting, soaked to the skin. Our helpless mother, hooked up to a morphine pump in her bed, was laughing too. I don't know what her friend made of it all, or even what we ourselves thought was going on. It was wildly euphoric, hysterical in every sense. We were in our twenties by then—my elder sister was even a mother herself—but the instincts of whoever flicked the first drops were perfect, for nothing other than that lunatic silliness could have brought this essential release from the exhaustion, from the numb, slow-motion grief that had occupied the house for so long. We needed it, in order to keep going. A terrible thing was befalling our family once again. But we were young, our mother was not dead yet. We were all alive, and to know that, to feel it bodily and celebrate it, was *allowed*.

Is the human impulse to laugh through tears always about this pressure release? Maybe. Maybe it's also a somatic expression of disbelief—a refusal to accept that what is before us can actually be happening. Or perhaps laughter at terrible times releases some badly needed hormone or brain chemical, pain relief for the soul.

Whatever the reasons, laughter and hurt are as inextricably linked in literature as they are in life. I think of Amy Bloom's sassy, bittersweet literary voice, or Sigrid Nunez's incisive, compassionate humour in novels like *The Friend* or *What Are You Going Through*. Nunez told me in an interview that she uses humour partly as a form of reader seduction. Her books often take human experience of great sadness as their subject—terminal illness, for example, or suicide. In that context, Nunez wants to offer her readers 'an element of lightness and playfulness' as a kind of gift. But she also does it for reasons of simple verisimilitude. In friendship, and even in life's darkest moments, Nunez says, 'there is no experience that doesn't have some comic element to it . . . the playfulness is always there. It's always there.'

It's not only in a book's subject matter that laughter can be found, but in form and language, even grammar and punctuation. Anne Enright articulated this beautifully when speaking to students at University College Dublin in 2017. She was describing the narrative voice of Gina, heroine of her novel about marriage and infidelity, *The Forgotten Waltz*.

> I tend to shift tone from paragraph to paragraph and sentence to sentence, and even sometimes on either side of a comma. You get a kind of ironic shift or lift, or you realise something was a bit of a joke but you're not quite sure what the joke was. Gina is . . . full of jokes, which isn't quite a sense of lightness, it's almost a sense of hurt, expressed as lightness, irony being a kind of distance you have from yourself or the situation. That remove, that disconnect, is not always a joyful one but it's quite a powerful one.

Enright seems here to be talking about voice as a manifestation of laughter through hurt; humour as analgesia.

Hurt is present, too, in another aspect of laughter—as defiance, as resistance. Here, thoughts turn most immediately to satirical writing—to dark political comedies like Joseph Heller's *Catch 22*, perhaps, or Kurt Vonnegut's *Slaughterhouse-Five*. But in thinking about social critique and laughter, I'm just as likely to turn to Jane Austen, and the way her wit so sharply exposed the injustices of the class and gender restrictions of her era. In contemporary Australian literature, I think of the work of Wayne Macauley, with his strange, black novels about social alienation and cruelty in the late-capitalist era. I think too of Michelle de Kretser's sharpened scalpel, and the incisions she makes into privileged, progressive thinking on race and class in books like *Questions of Travel* and *The Life to Come.*

Satire is often perceived as a rather chilly art form, some might even say cynical, but the best satire is born of deep optimism about the possibilities for human endeavour. It's just that those possibilities are so constantly squandered. As Anita Brookner said, 'Satire is dependent on strong beliefs, and on strong beliefs wounded.' Scratch a cynic, the saying goes, and you'll find a disappointed idealist.

I asked Wayne Macauley about the often bleakly funny version of Australia to be found in his fiction, and whether he'd ever been an idealist. He answered, 'I'm incredibly idealistic. That's the problem! If I didn't think about all the potential . . . I'd be very different. But I do have idealism—ridiculous, ludicrous idealism, when I think about it.'

Aside from satire, there's another, more surprising form of laughter as resistance that I first noticed in the fiction of Kim Scott. Scott, a Noongar man and two-time Miles Franklin winner, is very much aware of a sense of humour as a weapon in his work. It's wielded not as satire but a form of playfulness. I asked Scott about his books' capacity for joy even while speaking of monstrous cultural destruction and the most dreadful abuses of Aboriginal people. This is what he said about the humour in his second novel, *Benang*:

I knew what I was doing. I was trying to make fun of some of the really shitty stuff . . . it defuses some of the hurtfulness that's in there, I think, by playing with it. And it also seemed gutsy to play in that context. It seemed courageous—not only because it was difficult to sort of psych yourself up to do that, but because it might also be seen as an unworthy way to deal with nasty shit like that, to play with it. It is a source of such hurt and damage, you know, what are you doing playing? . . . [It's] not an appropriate response. But it seemed very necessary.

Along with music and dancing—two other manifestations of laughter, I'd suggest—these bubbles of optimism and joy play out again and again in Scott's work.

Bundjalung writer Melissa Lucashenko is another whose work depends on sharp humour for much of its power. Like Scott, Lucashenko is deliberate and defiant about this, and has spoken about humour as one of the four pillars of her work in exerting her sovereignty as a modern Indigenous woman. Her stories of contemporary Aboriginal people will always have these four elements: 'Beauty, Power, Humour and Land'. Even in the midst of literary truth-telling about hurt and shame and abuse, Lucashenko has written,

we should have those things on the page, or be working towards them. That's why I never kill off Black characters prematurely—the myth of the dying race is too strong, too powerful. We need to be alive on the page. We need to be fighting, and standing strong. We need to remember what allowed us to build the very first civilisation on this planet, our intelligence, our beauty and our pride in ourselves.

Laughter as courage, as taking charge of your own history and pushing back against oppression and stereotype by saying, '*I* decide what material I get to be playful with'—how magnificent, how profound.

Laughter is a generative, creative force. Just as anger can be fuel for art, laughter does the same work in a different way. It can operate as a key change in a dark work, bringing lightness into gloom and providing a balancing energy. I hope, for example, that the darkness or sadness in my novels is ameliorated for the reader not only by little blasts of beauty but by moments of comedy and lightness. In this way, laughter can provide a breathing space for the reader, a moment to gulp some fresh air and sunshine before plunging back into the hard stuff.

But there is also, in the creative process itself, a very important role for play, for mischief. It's this form of laughter that provides a crucial energy for art. Elsewhere I've called this mischief-making impulse 'overturning or disrupting'—a writer's urge to change tack, to throw a spanner in the works. It's that part of our creativity which behaves like a mischievous imp, moving through a narrative and flipping over our carefully constructed ideas and orderly scenes. For me, this is an essential and hugely energetic part of writing. It often comes from a sense of boredom with the work as it stands, even—sometimes especially—if the existing work is perfectly well made.

One of the writers I observed in my PhD study described the benefits of allowing a kind of reckless, rogue spirit to enter her work:

> I reckon the impulse to muck things up is a massively good impulse. When I get that little voice in the fiction, it's often the start of the real idea. It's the part of you that wants to make a silly face during a job interview. When that [impulse] comes . . . it can be really good, because you think, 'Oh, this is digressive and has nothing to do with anything'—but it actually turns out to be key.

Some of the most important discoveries I've made in my own work have arisen from this experimental urge to poke a hole in something, blow it up for the hell of it. As adults we often resist this impulse—disruption is seen as immature or childish, and it's the kind of instinct we're trained out of in adolescence. But it holds enormous creative potential.

George Saunders is a master of the mischief principle, that spirit at work in his tender absurdist stories, and in the devastating novel

Lincoln in the Bardo, where ghosts who do not understand they are dead live and yearn in the graveyard alongside President Lincoln's lost son. Saunders has alluded to the disruptive urge when speaking of the moment he decided to sample bits of real historical texts, edit them, rearrange them and insert them into his book: 'That was [a] moment of excitement and a little bit of transgression . . . something about the almost suspect nature of that got me excited . . . I've learned to trust that feeling. If I'm being a little dangerous or a little naughty or a little transgressive . . . then I know to go in that direction.'

I think many artists will recognise this sense of transgressive excitement in the creative process. It's like knocking over a glass of water to see what will happen. Writing against the grain of one's existing beliefs or instincts or knowledge often causes a sudden surge in energy that can reframe and inform and charge whole works with surprising new authority.

Humour has always been used to puncture inflated ideas, lampoon sentimentality or piousness. I think the kind of laughter I most enjoy in contemporary fiction is that expressed when the characters are behaving badly—especially if they are women. To a large degree, representations of women in popular culture still fall into the two restrictive categories of virtuous or vicious. In this context, for a writer to encourage good women to behave poorly feels like an act of liberation.

One of my favourite authors is Alice Thomas Ellis, an English writer who died in 2005 at 72 after producing a dozen novels. The *New York Times* described Thomas Ellis's fiction as 'unflinching dissections of middle class domestic life'. Often, what she's unflinchingly dissecting is the minutiae of relationships between women.

In her novel called (not so coincidentally) *Unexplained Laughter*, Lydia and Betty are staying at Lydia's weekend cottage in the Welsh countryside. Lydia has just been ditched by her unfaithful lover, and at a drunken office party has accidentally invited Betty, whom she doesn't much like, to stay with her in the cottage for the weekend. Now they're trapped there together, Lydia's loathing of Betty growing more intense by the minute. But Lydia was 'determined to be pleasant since the one thing more disagreeable than staying with someone you detested was staying with someone who detested you too. Dissembling was tiring but squabbling was disgusting. She would never be sufficiently intimate with Betty to quarrel with her.'

Lydia describes a visit by the Welsh builder, Emyr.

The sun shone the next day, and Emyr arrived to connect the water pipes. Betty made him a cup of tea and sat among the cut lengths of gleaming copper and strong-toothed tools conducting a little chat, which afforded Lydia a moment's amusement since Betty was adjusting her conversation to suit a person of low intelligence and the people of the valley were, on the whole, clever, devious and unusually literate. As Betty talked of the rain of the previous days the builder spoke briefly of water tables; as she deplored the unemployment of the Principality he gave a succinct resume of the economic situation; as, somewhat at a loss, she praised the sun for now shining, Emyr described in a few words how it would eventually burn itself out. The scene was rather like a bull-fight, with Betty, small-eyed, blundering hither and yon dazzled by the whisk of scarlet, the glancing slippers of the matador.

'What do you want for lunch?' enquired Lydia when Emyr . . . had left.

'I thought I'd make us my special salad,' said Betty. 'If you'll wash the lettuce I'll make my special dressing and we could pick some wild sorrel and chop it in at the last minute.'

'Do you know, I'm not hungry,' said Lydia, consideringly. There was something spinsterish in Betty's plans for her salad, something intimate in her expectation that Lydia would collude with her, and something repellent in the prospect of two single women fussing over food in the kitchen. Lydia was damned if she'd play salads with Betty.

I can't say exactly why this passage makes me laugh so much. Partly it's to do with the elegance of the prose, its musicality and verve. The image of bullish Betty—'small-eyed, blundering'—outsmarted by the working-class builder to whom she's trying to be condescending, is very funny. But to me it's Lydia's lavish, gratuitous meanness to Betty, and the self-hatred she unknowingly reveals in the process, that most enlivens this scene.

The upending of expectations is a well-known comic device— perhaps especially when they are beliefs or ideals that we most revere. But why does it bring a work so alive, make it so funny? I think it's to do with truth-telling.

Elizabeth Strout, the Pulitzer prize-winning author of *Olive Kitteridge*, among other books, has said interesting things about truth and laughter. When she first began writing, for a long time her fiction was rejected. After enduring this for many years, she had a hunch that this was because she wasn't being altogether honest in her work; there was something she was avoiding writing about. She'd always known that people laugh at something when it's true, so her rather unconventional response to this hunch was to enrol in a stand-up comedy class. What would happen, she wondered, if she put herself under the extreme pressure of stand-up before a live audience? What truths might pop out of her mouth?

The final exam involved performing at a New York comedy club, where she found her comic voice, sending herself up as 'this really uptight White woman from New England . . . I was just such a White woman and so much from New England that I didn't even know that about myself until I began to make fun of it. I was finally realising, oh, this is who I am.' After that, she began writing about an uptight White woman from New England, and her work took flight.

The electric delight of recognising difficult truths is strongest, it often seems, when what's being revealed is something shameful or ugly in human behaviour. When we reveal things that show us to be smaller, less worthy than we thought, we're making ourselves vulnerable. At points of revelation like these, laughter can be an extraordinary tool of connection. It allows us to see that we are all human; we are all children; we all fail. There's a sense of shared relief, immediately attended by a shared forgiveness.

My friend the writer and critic Tegan Bennett Daylight has taught creative writing in universities for many years. The first thing she tries to teach her students is to laugh at themselves. 'I ask them to cultivate a sense of humour as they write,' she once told me. In an echo of Strout's stand-up discovery, she said, 'When we're laughing at ourselves we're being honest about who we are—we're telling the truth.'

There's something profound in this. The ability to laugh at oneself reflects an openness, a flexibility of thinking. Laughing at yourself means acknowledging your fallibility. It shows you know you might be wrong.

I think this self-questioning is embedded in a writer's capacity for humour even if that humour is not visible on the page. In this form, the laughter is like a subterranean river of possibility and goodwill, flowing along beneath the work: you can't see it, but you feel the strength of its current beneath you as you read.

Is it too much of a stretch to believe that paying attention to this lightness, a sense of the possibility of a tonal shift, can allow us to face ourselves in other ways, to pause and question our own certainties?

It seems crucial now to examine our most fervently held beliefs anew—and to discover that sometimes we're wrong. Laughter has optimism and generosity embedded in it. As a generative force and an ethical choice, it's a refusal to accept that what we've done so far is irreversible, to accept that the world is unchangeable. I think that if we can imagine this refusal, we must enact it. If we can overturn an expectation, seize the power to play with dangerous material, if we can use laughter to tell difficult truths and harness it as a formidable creative force, we're acknowledging that things might not be as fixed as we thought.

When we laugh we drop our defences; our mood and perspective shift and lighten. If laughter lets us see that a moment was not what we thought it was, then we can imagine other aspects of our world to be different. We've done this as societies before—realised we were wrong about the 'threat' of women's suffrage or Black civil rights or marriage equality, say. We looked anew, stepped across the threshold to an unknown space to see what would happen. And found we didn't need or even want to keep to ourselves these rights we once thought impossible to share.

It's no coincidence that artists have always stood with those at the forefront of major social change: they know how to imagine. They know that if we can imagine a better world, then by a communal act of surrender—to uncertainty, to risk, to beauty—it might just be possible to bring it into being.

10

The Paint Itself

•————————•

The world inside a sentence

Scan the walls of any artist's studio or writer's room and you'll likely find an incantatory quotation or two from another artist, pinned up to inspire, provoke or console. Lately, mine seem to be coming from visual artists more than writers—like the American abstractionist Laurie Fendrich, who says the notion that abstraction is always about self-expression is both romantic and narcissistic. Abstraction can also be about ideas, she says: 'The complex struggle between order and chaos, for example, or how the flux of the organic world modifies the rigor of geometry.'

Something else Fendrich wrote struck me with great force: 'Ever since the invention of painting on canvas, paint itself has

122

been part of the meaning of a painting.' She was lamenting the pressure on young painters to offer explanations or narratives about their work, sometimes even before they had made it. This was a problem because meaning came, Fendrich asserted, not just from the artist's internal process, but from the actual application of the *paint*.

This may also offer the best explanation of what gives life to a piece of writing: meaning is generated in the application of language itself, rather than purely from the writer's desires or intentions, or from what they're writing about—the subject, the narrative. This truth is evident in any writing that pulses with brightness and energy.

I think novelist Lloyd Jones is referring to this when he quotes Beckett on James Joyce, as he occasionally does. Joyce's work, Beckett wrote, 'is not about something, it is that something itself'. When, in an interview, I asked Jones to elaborate, he told me: 'He's not writing about something—"about" suggests an object. In other words, it thrusts you into the task of describing something that's already there. But the something is emerging from the actual writing. So it's not starting with any objective in mind, but an objective actually results from the act of writing. It's a subtle distinction.'

Michelle Orange expressed this same distinction in a *New Yorker* review of Vivian Gornick's *The Odd Woman and the City*: 'Gornick's voice . . . does not just tell the story, it *is* the story.'

The paint itself is part of the painting's meaning; Gornick's and Joyce's words do not merely tell but are themselves the story, the real substance of their work.

It might seem obvious that a writer's paint is language, their brushstroke a sentence, but at a time when book publishing is increasingly inseparable from marketing, and when book clubs, literary prizes, social media and reviews seem to rely more and more on subject matter as the only reference point, what happens to a book whose language is its meaning?

If they're honest, I think every moderately successful literary writer knows that on some level they've just got lucky, happening upon a time and place in which their work has been able to slip through the usual barriers to economic viability. Often enough that luck has to do with their subject matter being easy to grasp, easy to talk about or argue with. I don't mean this is done cynically, or by intention; it just works out that way. I know, for example, that many of my peers have written far better but less easily marketable books than mine. The most talented among them might occasionally find themselves damned with that faint praise, 'a writer's writer'. It's not impossible for a writer's writer to find a wide readership—look at Alice Munro or George Saunders or Anne Enright. But there are so many others, overlooked because their work is hard to summarise in a cover blurb, because they don't fit neatly into sales categories, because their finest qualities cannot be articulated in any form except the experience of reading them. These are the authors I'll read every time they publish, no matter the subject. They're the writers I admire even when a book of theirs fails in more ordinary terms (plot, say, or characterisation), because their language is so compelling it becomes the story itself.

We seem to have forgotten how to talk about this, in public at least. Book reviewers, prize judges, booksellers and interviewers, even some publishers themselves—all sincere friends of books and writers—almost never mention language in public. They rarely speak of syntax or cadence, voice or pattern or even literary style, preferring to focus on subject matter and emotional affect, sometimes rounding off with a couple of vague catch-alls—like 'exquisite prose' or 'haunting lyricism'—that are already clichés in themselves.

I shouldn't find this approach so demoralising, because it's effective. Writers want readers, after all, and a review that hails the cadence of sentences or a delicacy of structure is—I suppose—less likely to entice than one detailing gripping plotlines or the author's heartbreaking back story or the outlandish lengths they went to in their research. But the effect of this focus on subject and storyline feels infantilising, as if literature is only worth something if any fourteen-year-old can appreciate it.

It's discouraging because I believe that when a good reader is enthralled by a book, even if they don't know it, it's not just the story but the sentences themselves that are responsible. And for many writers, those things we find ourselves endlessly talking about in public are the least interesting parts of making a book. Plot, event, research, narrative, theme, even character—to me these are the mechanical essentials one has to include in order to be allowed to play with the really interesting stuff. The language.

The work of a writer, day to day, is in playing with sentences. Weighing and balancing them, interrogating them for precision. And the focus on subject matter and theme—those topics that become shorthand descriptors, like *trauma* or *misogyny* or *ageing*—seems to miss the point of what art is really for.

So what's a writer's paint actually made of?

A friend and I recently taught a class called 'What makes a compelling sentence?', and in preparing for it we found ourselves in days of engrossing conversation, trying to work out the answer. We came together with piles of sentences we'd each chosen at random from the books around us, from writers like Colson Whitehead, Sayaka Murata, Alexis Wright, from Gerald Durrell and Martin Amis and Toni Morrison. We spent time together laying out these strings of words and looking hard at them, really looking, to unearth what it was *exactly* that made each of these sentences so alive.

In the end, we settled on five essential elements: clarity, authority, energy, musicality and flair.

Importantly, these elements were almost never to do with the kind of lyrical flourish readers often think of when remarking on 'beautiful sentences'. More often, their capabilities were expressed in perfectly ordinary vocabulary, sometimes even quite flat language. Many of our categories overlapped, and some had a whole series of subgroups. Some were almost ethical or moral at heart, and others more to do with mechanics and practicality. Clarity, for example, might be made up of economy, sincerity or truth, logic, and accuracy in grammar, spelling and punctuation (if you think this last is surely too basic to mention, take a look at any managing director's LinkedIn post and you'll quickly change your mind). Authority in a sentence, we thought, might involve a firmness of intention, trust in the reader's intelligence, a sense of movement, and risk. At its most exciting, the risk might be that the sentence (and thus the whole book) could even leave the reader behind: the authority rested in the author's willingness to take the sentence their own way, with or without us, the reader. Musicality, of course, is about the rhythm of language—its syntax and cadence, its ability to please the ear. (When an audience listening to a reading lets out one of those murmurs of satisfaction at the end, I'm convinced it's almost always in response to a pleasing rhythm.) But attention to its musicality shows a sentence as capable of so much more than melodiousness—rhythm alone can argue, preach, threaten, jolt or suffocate as easily as it can soothe or invigorate. The energy in a sentence might come from its voice, from mystery, from compression, reversal or surprise. As for flair, it's one of those qualities one can more easily recognise than anticipate, and a sentence with real flair could use various combinations of any of the above, or invent new ways of operation altogether.

When Katherine Mansfield begins 'The Garden Party' with, 'And after all the weather was ideal.', for example, there's both mystery and an energising movement already at work in its first three words. What does 'after all' refer to? What came before 'And'? Something important has already happened in this story, the reader senses, and we must scurry to catch up if we want to be a part of it. The sentence also holds a hidden threat (and thus, narrative urgency), because if the first words of a story so blithely assert how ideal things are, something must surely soon arrive to puncture that perfection.

Now consider the opening of Toni Morrison's *Beloved*: '124 was spiteful. Full of a baby's venom.' Feel the alienating risk of it—what on earth is 124, and how can a *number* be spiteful!? (It's a house, as it turns out, haunted by a furious dead baby, but we don't know this yet—we have to read on to find out.) Listen, too, to the rhythm of that couplet, snapping with all the percussive, even slightly aggressive, energy of a snare drum.

And so our explorations went. My friend and I took enormous delight in this discussion, which in the end revealed an obvious truth: the potential functions of a sentence are endless. We chose five elements, but in another week we could have chosen a different five and come up with a whole new set of essential traits of an effective sentence.

Aspiring writers are sometimes dismayed by this kind of talk. Some of them were dismayed by our discussion, I know. I think they're bored by an intensity of attention to what feels like such insignificant stuff, as if they're being asked to focus on the flakes of paint on a window frame when there's a dramatic view just beyond the glass. They've been trained by the market to think that the view—the subject matter, the narrative—is all that matters.

Before I met my husband, a musician, my appreciation of music was similarly blunted: I only ever really heard the dominant tune, or thought I did. If a familiar song played when we happened to be together I would sing along with the melody. But he, a brass player who has taught trumpet and piano, would be humming along to a whole different voice in the music – only the bass line, perhaps, or the brass chorus. Over time I grew to understand how little I'd noticed before, and that what was really affecting me so bodily in a favourite song had surprisingly little to do with the surface melody of a piece. Much more, I was pulled into a song by the underlying attraction of its harmonic and rhythmic structures and counter melodies.

But back to paint. In the BBC documentary *A Picture of the Painter Howard Hodgkin*, writer Colm Tóibín says that labelling

Hodgkin a 'colourist', as he was sometimes called, would be to use 'an offensive term'.

'He's a *painter*, and he happens to work, as all painters do, with colour,' Tóibín explains. 'But the paintings are not a way of making a wall pretty . . . It's so hard to describe because he's working very tactfully and sensitively off a nervous system, to tell you something that's absolutely crucial to him. But it's not something simple.'

Then Tóibín, his voice dripping with derision, makes me laugh out loud.

'Being called "a colourist" is a sort of nightmare. I think for a novelist it's like being called a *storyteller*. "Oh, he's a great storyteller." You know, you spend your life *shaping* things, forcing sentences into certain positions. Making a paragraph sharp. But they say, "Oh, he's a great storyteller." It's that sort of thing that really irritates . . .'

I think a writer who's bored by sentences might quite like being called a storyteller. But the ones I most respect would agree with Tóibín. And they'd agree with Francis Bacon, that maker of monstrous, dazzling, confounding pictures.

Bacon was frustrated by attempts to assign characters to or infer stories from the strange figures in his work, and repeatedly declared he had no interest in illustration or narrative. It wasn't so much that he deliberately wanted to avoid telling a story, he once said, 'but I want very, very much to do the thing that Valery said—to give the sensation without the boredom of its conveyance. And the moment the story enters, the boredom comes upon you.'

This is why I love listening to painters talking, and why they help me to write fiction. They make me remember what I really value in a work of art: the blow to the nervous system, the sensation freed from its mechanical conveyance.

The paint itself.

11

Reading Isn't Shopping

—————•—————

Why creativity needs disturbance

Some time ago, I found myself spending the weekend with a collection of pictures I didn't much like.

I'd volunteered as gallery attendant for a friend's group show. The paintings had been chosen by a renowned contemporary artist I loved, and I trusted his judgement—I knew that the works, many by highly respected painters, were understood by him and other gallerists and artists who visited the show to be 'good' pictures.

Nevertheless, many of them disturbed me. Not because the images were of disturbing things; they were portraits, abstract works and landscapes. So my unease was not to do with *what* they were, but rather how they were: the colours were often murky, or garish. Some

of the pictures looked to have been painted too quickly, felt unfinished to me. Sometimes the composition was inelegant. A few seemed
almost violent in their chaotic application of paint. Quite often they
were just too strange, too mysterious to me: I simply couldn't understand what the hell they were doing.

When I found two or three pictures I liked very much, the relief
I felt was substantial.

Ordinarily, when I see pictures I don't like in an exhibition, I just
walk on by and don't think about them again. When I see pictures I
love, I don't question why. But sitting there in the gallery in silence,
with nobody but the odd visitor stepping quietly through the space,
I had time to interrogate my conflicting feelings about these works,
to think about what was causing my unease, and my relief. What *was*
it that made me feel either good, or bad, on looking at these images?

One aspect of my discomfort was to do with the fact that people I
respected had judged these pictures to be good. I had to acknowledge
that beneath my dislike was a feeling of shame that they could see
something I couldn't. This led to a kind of loneliness, and a level of
anxiety. And I was alarmed to find that lying deep beneath all of this
was a distinct, fine but primitive layer of anger—anger born of the
fear of something I didn't understand.

After a little while, I realised that the level of either discomfort
or relief on first looking at an image was a result of how recognisable
the picture was to me in style, in subject matter. The ones I liked were

the kinds of paintings I have on my own walls at home. Interestingly, they were also generally the smaller works—perhaps more containable for me in some way, not only physically, but psychologically. The paintings I found most repellent, by contrast, were those most *unlike* what I might buy for my walls. They were huge, often dark, with a presence that felt almost hostile.

As I broke these feelings down, I was forced to confront that what was happening inside me was a kind of visual xenophobia. I don't know much about art, but *I like what I know.*

A few days after my duties as gallery attendant, I received an invitation to another group show in another gallery. This was an exhibition of landscapes, and I could see immediately that they were serenely beautiful. But when I looked through the catalogue of paintings, I was surprised to find something new at work in my consciousness. It was as though the so-called 'ugly' pictures had somehow entered me, and these new paintings, which I would ordinarily have liked very much, now seemed to lack some strength or energy. They were too calm, their colours and composition too familiar.

I realised I'd undergone some transformation in the presence of those other pictures. It seems that without the irritating stone of discomfort and disorder—even the strange, shameful anger that formed in me while I absorbed them—I could no longer find real pleasure in a tasteful, orderly painting. Looking at the new landscapes made me feel slightly tranquillised; there was a short-lived surge of initial pleasure as I saw, and recognised, and appreciated, but the feeling quickly faded, leaving an empty sort of outline. I can't now remember anything much about those images.

The whole experience made me want to take a closer look at what's going on when a work of art, a work of literature, has the capacity to make us 'feel bad', and how we respond to this as individuals, and as a culture.

§

That weekend was revelatory for me, but in fact I'd experienced this same turmoil before—the unease, confusion, even anger and disgust, followed by the hunger for those very emotions once they were gone. It was after my first visit to the Museum of Old and New Art (MONA) in Tasmania, where your own response to the work is the first response—there's no mediation or comforting description by way of sign or authoritative guide, and even if you seek out explanation using the museum's 'O device' (a digital gallery guide offered to every visitor), you'll find competing, contradictory interpretations— or sometimes none at all. The building itself, with its labyrinthine design, its darkness and tilting surfaces, intensifies the discomfort. The disquiet of having no way to locate your responses to the works is compounded by the feeling of not knowing exactly where your own body is in space.

If you have been to MONA, I imagine you may have felt the same things I did. I reeled in horror at the cruelty and violence of some of the works I saw there and wept, awestruck, at the beauty of others. When I left MONA, for some time every other gallery I visited seemed as anodyne and bourgeois as a department store. And it was a strange understanding that dawned on me when I had to ask: could I have experienced the awe if I had not also felt the horror?

§

Those who criticise David Walsh find his shock tactics cynical. They charge that his provocative collection, with its wall of ceramic vulvas, the videos full of puerile sexuality and violence, his giant shit machines and inverted Christian crosses, is born not of any sincere impulse towards examining the human condition but of nihilism. Walsh himself promotes this view, then denies it, then changes it again. (Even he, though, had to concede and apologise for the offensiveness of a recent Dark Mofo festival proposal that saw Spanish artist Santiago Sierra calling for Aboriginal Australians to donate their blood, which he would use to soak a British flag as a statement about colonisation. Among the thousands condemning the proposal was Indigenous rapper Briggs, who commented: 'We already gave enough blood.' The project was cancelled.)

I don't pretend to know what Walsh's motives are and I don't really care. But as a writer, I do think the question of motive in asking people to engage with a violent work of art is an important one. It's a personal question for me, because my novel *The Natural Way of Things* occupies some ethical territory I found extremely difficult to navigate. The matter of how to write about the exploitation of and violence against women without myself exploiting or causing psychic harm to women troubled me deeply. I drew certain lines for myself—ruling out graphic descriptions of violence, for example—though plausibility demanded that I write very close to, if not across, the edge of that line. I hoped I was treating this material sensitively, yet as I wrote, the novel seemed to demand that I be bold, even fearless, that I abandon sensitivities in favour of a tough statement.

It's not for me to say whether the novel manages to stay on the right side of the line, because I don't know where it is, and it moves for every reader. More than a few women have told me they're too frightened to read my book because of their own experiences of misogyny and violence. Some think the book would make them too angry, others too upset. I respect these decisions entirely. But other conversations have left me feeling rather more depressed.

One of these took place at a festival in Western Australia, where a doctor introduced himself to me, then confided that his friend, another man, had warned him not to read my novel 'because it's too gruesome'. I wasn't sure what he wanted me to say; I made an evasive noise and began looking for an exit. Then the doctor grinned and asked, with what felt to me like ghoulish relish, 'Well, *what's it about?*'

I didn't know how to answer; something in the way he asked his question bothered me. I said it was true the book was not a pleasurable read, because it was about women being mistreated. I must have looked as glum as I felt, because then he tried to cheer me up. 'Oh, but it's very fashionable to write about that sort of thing,' he said, 'so there must be *some* kind of market for it!'

Having thus encouraged me, he turned away and our conversation ended. But his words did not leave me, because they cut deep. Obviously I hate the idea of my book being 'too gruesome' for anyone to read—I'd hoped it had poetry and beauty along with the darkness—but more appalling was the suggestion that I deliberately sought out the degradation of women as a trending topic, in the certainty it would pull in a few bucks.

That exchange is the most recent example of someone implying that my motives were less than pure, but it's by no means the only one—plenty of others have more or less told me they shared this belief. A fellow writer once admonished me, saying she refused to read my book because she disapproved of 'trading in violence'.

Trading. Fashion. Market. These words all hurt, of course, because they're precisely the sickening motives I worried about so much as I wrote my book. Provocation for its own sake, titillation, violence as entertainment are anathema to me, and I tried hard, in the process of writing and in the content of the book itself, to avoid this very sensationalism. There are reviewers who've approvingly referred to my book as literary horror—that, too, concerns me, because (perhaps wrongly) I've always understood that genre to be characterised by the deliberate activation of fear and revulsion for its own sake. I like to think my motive was exploration, not exploitation, so the fact there are people who think I chased sensation or even merely failed in what I tried to do is painful.

But so what? I'm adult enough to know that trying to control what others think of you, or needing readers to believe in your good intentions, is not just a fool's game but an infantile one. And what's more important, I think, is to acknowledge to myself that as painful as it is, these sceptics might be right. It's possible my good intentions don't exist. My beliefs about my own practice, my motives and the result, could be entirely wrong.

§

Over the past decade, the word 'relatable' has come up in discussions about reading. 'Relatability' is a word that elicits a groan from those of us who see ourselves as sophisticated readers.

I've mostly heard 'relatable' said among book-club readers or festival audiences who use it as a compliment, to show they have connected with a work. A harmless shorthand, surely. But casual conversation isn't the only place 'relatability' is cited. University teacher friends report its widespread use in essays about books and reading even by postgrads, in subjects that are supposed to be about analysis and interrogation of literature.

It's easy to sneer, from the pages of literary magazines, at those readers who like books to be 'relatable'. But what's wrong with wanting to connect a book with one's own experience? Why exactly do we sneer?

It's worth teasing out what emanates from this word *relatable*, because I don't think it's as simple as it might first appear. And the sentiment, if not the word itself, is not expressed only by dummies and philistines.

As far back as 2014, Rebecca Mead was bothered enough by its use among journalists and film reviewers to write a *New Yorker* piece titled 'The Scourge of "Relatability"'. She was provoked by Ira Glass, the adored host of public radio program *This American Life*, who had emerged after a performance of *King Lear* to tweet, seemingly without irony: 'No stakes, not relatable . . . Shakespeare sucks!'

'To seek to see oneself in a work of art is nothing new, nor is it new to enjoy the sensation,' wrote Mead. 'Identification with a character is one of the pleasures of reading . . . though if it is where one's engagement with the work begins, it should not be where critical thought ends.'

There's a distinct difference, Mead claimed, between the active work of thinking myself into the experience of a character on the page—identification—and demanding that the *work* map itself onto *my* experience: 'If the concept of identification suggested that an individual experiences a work as a mirror in which he might recognize himself, the notion of relatability implies that the work in question serves like a selfie: a flattering confirmation of an individual's solipsism.' The onus of responsibility has shifted, Mead is saying, from a reader's capacity to thoughtfully interrogate how they might see themself in the work to a desire for the *book* to do the work for them, to hold off their appreciation or analysis until it first proves itself reflective of *their* life, their concerns.

'Relatability' might be a newish word, but I don't think the temptation to deem a book worthy because it's recognisable is new. I clearly remember my country high school English teacher banning the words 'because I can relate' from our classroom. Whether we related or not, whether we *liked* a book or not, was of absolutely no relevance, she told us. The question, then, was what is the work doing on its page? What else might we find, if we look more closely, ask better questions?

My question now is, if sixteen-year-olds were being trained out of this so many decades ago, why is the same impulse so prevalent among adults now?

I think it has to do with the explosion of consumer culture since my long-ago high-school days. We live now in a world where our every interaction is followed by a request for a star rating, a thumbs-up or thumbs-down. We've been slowly but thoroughly trained to see the world in terms of its capacity to please us, and however romantic we might be about books, it's naive to expect reading to remain somehow quarantined from this customer service perspective.

Indeed, these days we're asked to rate our satisfaction out of five stars not only after an Uber ride or a hotel stay, but following a performance at our major theatre companies. More than one publisher's books come with promises of a 'Fantastic read or your money back!' This kind of promotion, usually for mass-market fiction, urges readers to accompany refund requests with 50–100 words 'detailing why you didn't enjoy the book'.

Even in so-called literary works, it's not uncommon to find a list of helpful questions and 'topics for discussion' when you turn the last page of the novel, such as the list in my edition of Elizabeth Strout's *Olive Kitteridge*. (Question one: 'Do you like Olive Kitteridge as a person?' Question two: 'Have you ever met anyone like Olive Kitteridge, and if so what similarities do you see between that person and Olive?') Before I had time to exhale after the book's final sentence, let alone reflect on what it meant, the publisher's marketing department was there to help me form my thoughts.

All of this, quite evidently, is in the pursuit of higher sales. I'm not entirely blaming publishers here, for with author incomes at record lows, it would be a brave writer who resisted such efforts to bring more readers to their work. And yet there's something so disturbing about the incursion of these marketing tendrils into the pages of the book itself, that resist I think we must. Something dangerous is taking place in this seemingly benign quest for wider readership.

Nowhere have I been asked to rate anything on its capacity to make me uncomfortable, to unnerve or challenge or confuse me. And the prompt for rating—the anxious question, 'Did you like it?'—often arrives moments after the 'consumption' takes place. What if I were asked to think about what I've experienced and respond in a month, a year, a decade? It's unthinkable.

What does the publisher, the theatre company, *do* with these ratings, with the 50–100-word complaints? What does money-back 'customer satisfaction' mean when it comes to art?

Increasingly, I think 'reader satisfaction' is code for the smoothing out of lumps and bumps of every kind in pursuit of a soothing digestibility.

One sort of bump is evoked in requests for book recommendations routinely seen on social media, asking for 'uplifting, relaxing, entertaining reads—nothing sad or heartbreaking, please'. Any glance at a Facebook book club will show you the overwhelming appetite for novels in which nothing bad happens, especially to animals.

I'm not suggesting, by the way, that a book filled with degradation or misery is inherently superior to one full of cupcakes and potato-peel pies. My Western Australian doctor's remark stung precisely because it hit a nerve of potential truth. Depending on how it's done, a novel full of misogyny and violence from the shelf marked *Political* can be exactly as banal as any pink-jacketed goo from the *Heartwarming/ Relatable* section.

A related but separate lump that bothers many readers is uncivilised behaviour by fictional characters. Writers hear complaints from readers all the time about our characters' attitudes, their diets and laundry habits, their refusal to get therapy, their swearing. It's undeniable that a great many readers (and even some publishers) seem to have a need to morally approve of characters, to *like* them, before they find a book satisfying.

In a *Guardian* essay on teaching literature to university students, the writer Tegan Bennett Daylight described the surprising conservatism of her students. They were not only affronted by the explicit sex, drug-taking and poor parenting they saw in Helen Garner's *Monkey Grip*, and offended by 'graphic descriptions of sex and masturbation' in the work of Christos Tsiolkas, they found the *anger* of Tsiolkas's young queer Greek protagonist, Ari, intolerable. Daylight couldn't help but see in this a connection between consumerism and reading. On a good day, she hoped her students' disapproval was because they themselves were generous and happy people. But on a bad day, she wrote, 'I think they find Ari difficult because the distinction between adults and teenagers has been blurred. We all want the same things now: phones, clothes, and food to photograph. We are all consumers. Teenagers don't want to stick it to the man anymore. They *are* the man.'

Quite a few readers have complained to me, or among themselves, that people in my books behave poorly, or aren't fair representations of a certain demographic. One woman wrote that she had hated *The Weekend*—a novel about three irritable older women friends—because although she and her friends were of the same age, 'these women are nothing like us'.

Another wrote to tell me she'd wanted to read my book but changed her mind when she heard that one of the fictional characters was in a relationship with a married man. Did I not know how much hurt such women caused to others? This correspondent's raw pain radiated through the lines of her email as she went on to detail her own husband's infidelity, but, interestingly, she laid the blame squarely on the woman involved—not quite completely absolving her husband, but almost. I sympathised with her, but was also a little dumbfounded that she needed to reprimand a complete stranger over the morals of an unread book.

Many readers were appalled that the young jailed women in *The Natural Way of Things* were not more supportive of each other. Other novels of mine have been described as focusing on 'dysfunctional' families and 'loser' protagonists. To be fair, many readers have also responded to the novels because of, rather than despite, those same character flaws. But this points to another common response: the tendency for some readers (and many aspiring writers) to summarise characters' personalities in pseudo-psychological or actual diagnostic terms, like 'commitment phobia', 'dysfunctional', 'post-traumatic stress disorder' and so on.

Some editors even fall prey to this reading-as-therapy phenomenon. One editorial report I received for *The Children*, a novel about family disharmony, expressed irritated disapproval that the mother and adult daughter didn't have a more cordial relationship (hello?), while another editor's report on a friend's tender novel berated the author for her main character's middle-aged passivity. The fact that the central theme of the novel was the lifelong paralysis caused by grief seemed to pass the editor by. Both reports suggested remedies for making the characters better—nicer?—people. Both were ignored.

What's behind this kind of therapising reading? Perhaps it's an attempt to corral and pin down human behaviour in these terms in the belief it will help a reader understand people. Or is it an opposite impulse? Is it that once a character is diagnosed in such a way, one might be free from the obligation to think or engage any further? If all behaviour is just part of a quasi-medical syndrome, separated out from ordinary human existence, we can more easily put distance between a character's ugliness and failures and our own.

It's easy to be snooty about readers who want characters to be nice, or psychologically healthy. More troublesome to the politically minded reader, it seems to me, is the situation when *no clear diagnosis* of a character's moral malaise is offered by the writer. 'Problematic' is the new code word here. Ambivalence or contradiction is worrying, and best avoided. A fellow writer sternly told a novelist friend of mine that she didn't know *what* to think about the latter's Aboriginal character. My friend took that as a compliment. It wasn't meant as one.

Mystery and weirdness is another lump that gets in the way of guaranteed reader satisfaction. I don't only mean hints of the otherworldly, or signs that something stranger is happening than first meets the eye—although to me those little hints at other layers of meaning are often what make a work of fiction sing. But the more I go on, as a reader and writer, the more I'm also drawn to unconventionality in the shape and mechanism of a story, to structural and narrative strangeness. While I still have the greatest respect for the traditional, linear narrative arc, I'm increasingly beguiled by stories and writers who abandon it—something I'm perhaps still too afraid to try myself. How, I wonder, would a book like Alexis Wright's *Carpentaria* fare in the 'Fantastic read or your money back' offer? How would George Saunders's *Lincoln in the Bardo*, or even Elizabeth Strout's *My Name is Lucy Barton*? That these novels are lauded is testament to a community of readers and publishers prepared to venture with writers into new, almost anti-narrative, territory. But this community is small, and shrinking, and if any of these books had been a first novel by an unknown writer, I doubt the response would have been the same.

§

I said earlier that it's easy to sneer at those lesser beings who want books to be uplifting or relatable, but my experience with the paintings, in which I discovered in my own response to the visual arts an attitude I'd find contemptible in a reader, suggests that even if we think we're more sophisticated than that, few of us are free from an instinctive desire to smooth and flatten out, to diagnose and close the file. It's natural to want to alleviate discomfort by making knowable what is unknown. And even if we're too good for 'relatability', many of us are addicted to what Aleksandar Hemon has called 'epiphany peddling and empathy porn'.

Like 'relatable', the word 'empathy' has been a watchword in talk about books for some time now. I've probably used it myself. Empathy is everywhere. In his endlessly quoted defence of libraries, for example, the writer Neil Gaiman said, 'A book is a little empathy machine. It puts you inside somebody else's head. You see out at the world through somebody else's eyes. It's very hard to hate people of a certain kind when you've just read a book by one of those people.'

Barack Obama said something similar in his conversation with the novelist Marilynne Robinson. Setting aside being president, he told the author,

> the most important set of understandings that I bring to the position of citizen, the most important stuff . . . I've learned from novels. It has to do with empathy. It has to do with being

comfortable with the notion that the world is complicated and full of grays, but there's still truth there to be found, and that you have to strive for that and work for . . . the notion that it's possible to connect with some[one] else even though they're very different from you.

It's hard to argue against this. Surely the discovery of common ground between you and an enemy can only be a force for good, for connection, for harmony? The trouble is the assumption that common ground is always there to be found. And the more I think and read about this, the narrower the gap seems between laudable empathy and contemptible relatability.

Sarah Sentilles is one writer who has argued compellingly against our deification of empathy. The author of *Draw Your Weapons*, a meditation on art, war and ethics, Sentilles says that the embrace of 'unknowable otherness', rather than empathy, is our society's most urgent task. Drawing on the work of theorists and philosophers including Judith Butler and Emmanuel Levinas, Sentilles writes: 'Empathy depends on perceived likeness, a sense of sameness; I treat you justly because I recognize you as fundamentally like me.' But, she goes on, 'if it's only discovered likeness that creates the possibility for ethical behaviour, what happens when likeness can't be found? . . . In this climate of fear and oppression, something more radical than empathy is needed. The faith that deep down "they" are like "us" won't get us where we need to go. Because what if they're not like us at all? What then?' The difficult task Sentilles sets us about ethics is 'to learn to live with, and protect, what we can't understand'.

Aleksandar Hemon issues the same challenge in the world of literature. In an argument for reading Proust, he wrote: 'We have to adjust, or even abandon, our habitual expectations and submit to a transformation we cannot fully control . . . But the reward of finding our way in that new space, of figuring what is in it, of allowing the discovery to change our thought, far exceeds merely recognizing and confirming what we already know.'

But even here, we need to resist epiphany or resolution, because if what I'm saying is true—that the unknowable and uncomfortable, the *friction* of these things, is the grit that gives birth to the pearl— I must also accept that there's a strong chance the grit may always remain grit. The pearl may never form, the hard work might yield no reward at all.

And yet, I do believe, and very powerfully, that somehow the hard work *is* its own reward. It's the pushing against opposition, the attempt to solve the potentially unsolvable, that creates some inner expansion hard to describe. But I think it's the feeling I had after MONA and my gallery experience: some flowering of a greater range of possibility for thought, for experience, that could only come from the struggle itself.

§

The most pleasing way to end this chapter would be for me to return to the show of paintings I presented at the start and elucidate the lessons they've taught me. I'm not being facetious, for I have learned things from them: that feeling lost or ashamed in the face of art might be natural, for example. They've reminded me that reading isn't shopping, that narcissism must be resisted—but also that one might occasionally do well to check one's own glass walls for cracks.

In this version I might present those pictures again to show how they no longer look unpleasant to me, how in examining my own responses I've come to a new understanding that reveals the works to be shining, in fact, with a tough new beauty.

But now we're at the end and I'm looking at the pictures again— and I still don't like them. I still find some of them ugly; I still don't understand what they're doing. But in their 'radical otherness' they have forced me to think, and that is suddenly more transcendent and precious than beauty. I'm released from dull egotism, from the childish demand that I should always get what I want—and it's the difficulty itself that shines.

12

The Outside Voice

In praise of unruly artists

A fellow novelist once said about me, approvingly, that I'd 'gone feral'. He was talking about *The Natural Way of Things*, and I took his remark to refer to the furious tone of the book as well as one of its characters, who actually turns half animal. But I secretly hoped it was also a description of my creative self, because if it was, it might be the greatest compliment I would ever receive.

Feral: untamed and wild, escaped from domestication, damaging to the status quo, destructive, invasive, unruly, disobedient. For a female artist, what's not to love?

When I think of the artists I most respect, those I call up as imaginary guides on the days my confidence falters and I feel small, many of them are women whose work might also be described as untamed, who have stepped away from social expectations of being nice or good. Turning feral to me means an artist has entered the unknown, unexplored places. It means they've broken free in some way—and even if they return to the ordinary world, that re-entry is on their own terms: they've internalised unruliness and brought it back, inside themselves, to stay.

It's a truism to say that artists are always outcasts in some way. I once read some research showing that no matter how much we claim to embrace creativity and want it in our lives, most people and organisations actually do the opposite—we fear and actively work to reject creativity when we see it. Even if we insist otherwise, what we actually want is replication of established, previously approved forms of 'originality'. We don't want truly creative stuff in our lives, our homes or our workplaces, because it is too risky, always on the knife-edge of failure. It's new by definition, and thus unknown. The unknown is always a threat.

Unruly artists take to all this eagerly; they find a home in outsiderness. But while history has always made a certain space available to feral men, from Caravaggio to Picasso to Prince, feral women have a harder time of it. Much of our battle is internal. Raised from birth to please, to be helpful, to shrink and be decorative, for a woman to proudly show herself in all her individuality is a much greater challenge.

Even in artistic circles, female artists and writers are still rewarded for being attractive and agreeable, or else for being somehow wounded or afflicted. While this is slowly changing, I think an expression of sheer joy and strength in the work of women artists—most especially if they ignore men altogether—can still often be perceived as somehow trivial, unseemly or even embarrassing.

Well, as my filthy, rabbit-skin-clad character Yolanda might say, fuck that.

An important postscript to the research showing true creativity to be unwelcome is another finding: this rejection is *good for creativity*. Social rejection, it turns out, promotes imaginative thought. If women are doubly constrained by societal expectations, might it not follow that being outcast is doubly good for women's creativity, if they are strong enough to withstand the opprobrium?

When I call up those who inspire me artistically, I often think of women much bolder than I, whose painting and performance and music and writing and sculpture is unexpected and bracing. These are women who couldn't care less if I liked their work, or whether they fit in with others. Who answer only to the call of their own artistic ideals. Who may develop an admiring following, only to shuck it off when their interest leads them elsewhere. Who refuse to be anybody's poster girl for anything. Who look to the long game. Who have never considered gratitude or good behaviour a route to anything worth pursuing.

I think of women like sculptor Rosalie Gascoigne, who held her first exhibition at age 57, after the lessons she learned in ikebana floral art classes turned her feral. She used to 'drag branches and bits of old tin into the house' and horrify the neighbours, she said. '"Get her," they used to say. "Get her, look at that, look at that dirty thing she's got on her mantelpiece."'

I think of Wiradjuri artist Karla Dickens, whose mixed-media works of sly, raw power are made from found and discarded objects—from dog muzzles and straitjackets to emu feathers, ribbons, colourful toys, boxing gloves, fencing masks, furniture and fabric fragments. Her work is playful, sinister, celebratory and surprising.

Then there's Frenchwoman Sylvie Guillem, hailed as the greatest dancer in the world until she quit with a farewell world tour in 2015. Coming to dance from Olympic-level gymnastics, she was routinely called a 'physical freak' and earned the nickname 'Mademoiselle Non' because she declined to blindly do as she was told. 'We are talking about expression, feelings, freedom, something that is big,' she said in her final year of dancing. 'Don't restrain me by telling me that you have to express "like this". So I had a lot of fights with that. It was quite fun.'

Waanyi woman and author Alexis Wright is possibly Australia's most adventurous, most untamed writer yet. With her loose, operatic, surreal novels *Carpentaria* and *The Swan Book* and her 'collective memoir' *Tracker*, a communally constructed portrait of Aboriginal leader 'Tracker' Tilmouth, she has departed from Western storytelling modes altogether and is inventing a thrilling new form of literature, a particularly Aboriginal one, taking in ancient time and the contemporary world at once.

'Deeper in my mind, where the rational part of the brain weighs up what was really likely to happen to ambitious thoughts,' she's written of the creation of *Carpentaria*, 'I realised that this book might never be published because of the narrative storytelling style. This is the fear of taking risks and what you have to constantly fight against, to believe more than being fearful, that you are doing the right thing whatever the odds.'

Sydney sculptor Linde Ivemey is another artist of undomesticated ambition and expression. She uses the bones of chickens, fish, stingray, wallaby, goat and other animals, along with hair, viscera, suede, teeth, sacks and other materials to create her menacingly beautiful, playful yet nightmarish creatures. They might be half woman, half rabbit, or half bird, half jester. Ivemey makes sinister saints and hooded, grass-faced explorers and whimsical families with tusks and tiny handbags, and all of it is mesmerising, enchanting and unnerving.

Sometimes, among my inspirations, the rebellion is more directly visible in the woman herself than in the art she makes.

Monaro painter Lucy Culliton is someone I think of as wild at heart, though her work has been described as 'old fashioned' in its dedication to still life and landscapes, and because of her thoughtful composition and disciplined practice. I agree with critic John McDonald's assessment of her as 'that rare phenomenon: a natural painter. She proceeds from instinct, choosing her subject matter spontaneously, never letting go of a motif until she has exhausted every option. This kind of ability cannot be taught, as it springs from a deep part of the artist's personality.'

Culliton's choice of oddments and the overlooked for her still-life subjects—spark plugs, can openers, electric fans, old chair castors and weeds as often as flowers—shows up her rebellious streak. As do her portraits, which are more often of sheep, pigs or dogs than people.

Her paintings are often extravagantly coloured, wanton and ebullient, without a trace of irony or world-weariness. Against the ennui of the hip contemporary art world, Culliton's sincerity comes as a shout of radical delight.

Abstract expressionist Ann Thomson told me that when she was a young painter with her first solo show in 1965, the notion her gender might be an obstacle never occurred to her. 'Why would it? I was an artist! And I related to the great artists! I didn't think whether they were men or women, I just thought they were the great people who did what I wanted to do.' Later, a dawning realisation that her male contemporaries were receiving more attention than she brought the perils of self-consciousness: 'You start to *think* of yourself as a woman—and it's a shame. So then you think, well, I'm not going to indulge in that. I'm an artist, and that's what I do. That's that.'

Where's the common ground for these artists? What is it that bestows them with the disruptive authority they share?

First, I notice, they're often funny. Even if they are making work about difficult experiences or ideas, they make play with them, laugh at them, kick them around. The laughter might be dark, they might sometimes be laughing through tears, but these women make mischief with the hard stuff, and that's a powerful way of transforming pain into art.

Something else I've noticed is a simple self-acceptance in the way they speak. In interviews or in person, there seems no trace of self-consciousness or timidity about aspects of their work that other people might find outlandish. Instead, these women present their preoccupations and ways of seeing and expressing themselves—whether it's casting underpants in aluminium and adorning them with emu feathers or fishing lures or barbed wire, as Dickens has done, weaving chicken neckbones into a kind of chainmail armour like Ivemey, or Guillem's scuttling like a praying mantis across a stage—as absolutely logical and ordinary.

I think they also share a deep affinity with the natural world, sometimes overtly, in the work itself, and sometimes in the artist's own kinship with places, animals and plants. Culliton's home in particular is full of animals—her property is home to fourteen emus along with eight dogs, a number of horses and sheep, chickens and ducks, pigeons and other birds galore. A baby goat leaps onto her dining table and eats the flowers from her vases.

A rowdy, animal spirit is at work in all these artists, in their embrace of the down-and-dirty natural world: body parts and earth and weeds and rusted, discarded things, the things ordinary people try to conceal or eliminate, or find shameful or disgusting. In form, in subject, in their intellectual force and ambition, the feral artist doesn't merely tolerate but celebrates the primal, creaturely instinct in us, too—the rude, excessive, illogical and disorderly, primitive and urgent life force.

As Thomson says, that's that. That's what turning feral means for these women: *I'm an artist, and that's what I do.* It means a truly independent mind. It might mean ignoring your gender. It definitely means being open to surprise, being honest. It means embracing our own ugliness, our grubbiness and animality, without shame. It means releasing yourself from the desire to make people like you. It means having the guts to show yourself; discovering who and what you are, and expressing that self in whatever way you choose.

All of this inspires and energises me. The wildness of these artists gives their work something else too, something we don't talk about much in art. It's love. Their work is loved but it also *loves*, freely and abundantly, without hiding or self-protection. These artists have liberated themselves, and in so doing set their work free, allowing it to fully unfurl its wings and take flight.

13

Afraid of the Dark

• ———————— •

Anger as creative fuel

At a bookshop event one evening, a tall, well-dressed woman in her 70s hovered at my signing table for a long time.

The discussion had centred on my novel about misogyny. After these events, readers often come and talk with me. It's mostly a friendly affair, though sometimes it's confusing, or frightening. People tell me things that have happened to them. Women have asked me for help in getting the police to believe them. Occasionally one wants to punish me for what I've written or said, leaning in with a smile to deliver a subtly vicious insult she knows nobody but me will hear.

The woman on this particular night was not like these. She hung back, but stayed; something was bothering her. She picked up a copy of my novel and held it, turning it over and over, almost caressing it, as I signed others' books and chatted to them. Eventually she was the only person left, but still she hesitated. She wanted to read this book, she told me. She really did. She held it for so long without buying it I could feel annoyance beginning to radiate from the bookseller beside me. Finally, it came out. Bad things had happened to her when she was young, she murmured. And she was worried that if she read my novel, well, the anger would be . . . overwhelming.

I gently took the book from her, put it back on the pile, and told her I understood. I said she should not read it now, probably not ever. She seemed relieved. I won't forget the look I'd seen on her face. It was fear, of drowning in her own rage.

§

When I think of my early childhood, the most constant emotion I remember is anxiety about 'getting in trouble'. This had nothing to do with reality: my parents were loving, I was a compliant child, and apart from the chaos and daily skirmishes of siblinghood in a family of five kids, I was rarely 'in trouble' at home or at school. Nevertheless, my memory is of *fearing* that trouble—by which I mean admonishment, embarrassment, punishment, shame—would engulf me at any moment.

One of my sisters recently told me that for a time when I was a baby, my mother pinned a little handwritten note on my pram that said: *Please don't talk to me*—because if someone did, I would burst into terrified tears.

Surely this cannot be true.

The one emotion I don't recall feeling in my childhood is anger.

That can't be true either.

§

In Elizabeth Strout's novel *Anything is Possible*, 78-year-old Mary 'felt the kind of electrical twang that meant she was suddenly very angry . . . She had never liked being angry; she didn't know what to do with it.'

Strout's books are full of women who carry a force of dark and furious energy inside themselves. In some, like Mary, the darkness is buried deep; when they feel it rising to the surface they're afraid, or bewildered. But in Strout's most famous creation, Olive Kitteridge, the fury lies close to the surface, on a constant, dangerous simmer. The best-loved scene in both the book *Olive Kitteridge* and the HBO television series is the one in which Olive steals a bra and a single shoe from her hated new daughter-in-law's bedroom and defaces her expensive sweater with a magic marker before folding it neatly and returning it to its shelf.

Strout doesn't know where this episode came from, she told a BBC book club. She'd never done such a thing herself nor known anyone who had. 'But I will tell you this,' she said. 'Many people have come up to me when I'm on the road with this book, and they've said, "How did you *know*?"'

She also said of creating this scene in which an old woman takes childish, preposterous revenge on someone she despises: 'I mean, it was just so *fun*.'

Helen Garner shows a similar delight in her essay 'The Insults of Age', with its notorious scene in which the then 73-year-old author darts up behind a schoolgirl who has just deliberately frightened another older woman in the street, and gives the girl's ponytail 'a sharp downward yank'. After years of enduring society's affronts to ageing women, Garner finds that 'the shield of feminine passivity . . . splintered into shards'. She goes on a truth-telling spree, firing back insults to bar staff, shouting on planes, snapping at patronising publicists. The hide of her! As I read this gleeful exercise in comedy laced with black truth, a kind of illicit joy fizzled through me.

In these stories Olive does, and Helen does, what many of us are apparently longing to do: behave badly, even violently—and get away with it.

§

When I was around seven, my father read Norman Lindsay's *The Magic Pudding* to me at bedtime. Despite my older sister's and my usual resistance to books and TV shows that had, as we put it, 'no girls in' (for even as small children we had figured out there was something wrong with a world that assumed we didn't exist), I adored *The Magic Pudding*. I loved pugilistic Bill Barnacle and his friend Sam Sawnoff, the Penguin Bold. I was comforted by the presence of gentlemanly Bunyip Bluegum, but most of all I loved the Puddin' itself. Albert, the cut-and-come-again Magic Pudding, was rude, angry, gloomy, resentful, disobedient, violent and self-pitying—and at the same time enormously powerful. Lindsay's black-and-white illustrations were full of the same wild energy as his story, and I was enthralled.

When two of my nieces were small, their favourite TV show was *Super Nanny*, the 'reality' program in which useless parents were rescued from their children's wildness by bossy nanny Jo Frost, who trained the parents in discipline and household harmony. My nieces would sit on the floor, cross-legged and saucer-eyed, transfixed by the chaos exploding on screen. It was the unfettered rage of other children that gripped them: children with the nerve to refuse bedtimes and food, who spat and screamed and hurled abuse and objects—and whose parents appeared *powerless to stop them*. The havoc these television kids wreaked with their fury was as exhilarating to my nieces as the Magic Pudding's was to me.

But maybe the nieces and my girl self were entranced, too, by something deeper in these displays—something we intuited about growing up into women, about the world and its rules against anger for girls. Maybe we knew we were witnessing something we would never be allowed to express.

§

When people talk to me about *The Natural Way of Things*, the A-word always comes up. Journalists ask it earnestly, almost sadly, and so do readers: 'Are *you* angry?'

It feels as if I'm supposed to say no, that saying *yes* will somehow let the side down, get us all in trouble. It's demoralising, even now, how strong is my urge to shove that word away, to stuff it down. I prevaricate and qualify, I put limits on it, I talk about 'a range of feelings'. I try replacing it with other words people have used about my work. 'Ferocious' or 'fierce' or 'provocative' I can embrace, even feel proud of. But when it's within striking distance of women, 'angry' remains deeply, primitively shaming. As for my being 'too angry'—an observation made in disappointed tones and, publicly at least, only by women—that's the worst crime of all.

Once, an unsmiling woman of around 60 approached me, nodding in fervent recognition. She said with savage pride, 'I'm an *angry woman, too.*' And she was. Her eyes gleamed with a complicated, bitter fury. The muscles in her neck were rigid; I could feel the force of her breath as she spoke. I was so unnerved by her obvious anticipation of my approval that I'm afraid I laughed and made a joke.

If I'm honest, I was repelled. *You're on your own, lady*, I wanted to say. *I'm not in your club.*

But I must be in her club, mustn't I?

§

A snippet of news comes on the TV while I'm getting ready to go out. A veiled young Rohingya woman murmurs her story to a reporter. She was gang-raped by fifteen soldiers; three weeks later her internal injuries have not healed. Her husband has said he'll leave her if she doesn't stop bleeding soon.

I feel sick. I stop before the screen, my hand over my mouth.

Moments later I put on my lipstick and go out to a nice restaurant for dinner.

How is it possible that I do this?

Her quiet voice, the soft eyes, the downcast gaze. Her name is Noor. In the reporter's summary of her story, and all the others like it, the word 'trauma' is used, over and over. But what, I want to know, is a woman like Noor supposed to do, for the rest of her life, with all that *rage*?

§

Eimear McBride, the author of *A Girl is a Half-Formed Thing*, was asked why her protagonist's mother does not protect her daughter.

167

McBride said that, in Ireland at least, one of the Catholic Church's great triumphs was that 'it taught women to devour themselves'.

'When men feel anger, they *express* anger,' said McBride. 'When women feel anger, they feel guilty. So they turn it on themselves, and on each other.'

Guilt and anger, anger and shame.

Olive Kitteridge, says Elizabeth Strout, is consumed by both: '[She has] so many levels of rage, guilt, the whole thing . . . if she was a New Yorker she would have gone to therapy and blabbed her head off and joined a support group—but that's not what happens for this type of person, in Maine.'

I once joked in public that 'without shame we would have no art'. A woman in the audience took issue with this; she seemed appalled I could say such a thing. She had no shame, she declared, about anything. Why on earth would I want to celebrate it? We were out of time, I felt accused, and—coward—I evaded the question. What I should have said is this: that for many artists, this buried sense of difficulty, the presence of something unspeakable, or contradictory, or somehow 'bad' inside themselves is the pilot light for their best work. For Jonathan Franzen it's his messy feelings about family and marriage. He calls it his 'hot material'.

Writers do go on a lot about shame.

Here's something I've noticed. In the beginning, and for a long time, an artist can be most embarrassed by the very thing—sometimes the only thing—that gives their work life and verve. You're ashamed of it because you don't see it in other people's work. For a while, you do everything you can to bury this thing, disguise it, smooth it over. You long to be rid of it because you want to write a book like those you admire, those that are real; the opposite of yours. You're ashamed of this thing because it reveals the truth of who you are.

Sometimes, eventually, you can accept it and make use of it. Sometimes, later, you're ashamed because you're sick to death of it.

Who wants to *think* any more about women's anger? Who wants to see another hashtag, to learn the sordid details of yet another revolting encounter, hear another pathetic, self-serving apology? Who the hell is not yet bored to tears by the misery and injustice and *waste* of it all?

And yet there it is, the fury: forcing its way out, bursting up, unresolved, primitive, mighty.

As George Saunders said, 'You can choose what you write, but you can't choose what you make live.'

§

I was interviewed some time ago for a young American feminists' podcast. The same episode featured author Margaret Atwood, and it was poignant to hear, lying just beneath the young interviewer's questions, a search for guidance on how to manage her own feelings. When, she asked, had Atwood last felt angry?

Atwood replied, in her slow, low, gravelly Canadian voice—that voice always just on the edge of merriment—'You mean mildly peeved, or really raging?'

Raging, the young woman said. She meant that fury you feel when you watch the news, or you experience things in your personal life: 'I mean the anger that you feel in your *body*.'

Atwood had to think for a moment. She was not often angered these days, she said. Mostly she was surprised, or puzzled. 'I have to tell you this,' she said. 'After a certain age, you're not as easily triggered. You're calmer.'

'Really?!'

The young woman sounded incredulous, as if a future in which she might be released from her own anger was inconceivable.

§

Deep in my own middle age, I've taken to a fascinated observation of women belonging to the generation or two ahead of me. I'm aware that I'm uncomfortably watching my future self.

I wrote something in my notebook, one fictional old woman observing another:

There were different breeds of women. This one was of the crow variety. Steel-grey hair like a nun's, cheap, unflattering glasses, a watchful, vengeful expression . . . Crow women carried some deep anger inside themselves. It came out in the way they gripped the wide shoulder straps of their bags, in the rigid set of their mouths. It showed in the way their faces said, 'I dare you,' to everyone from waiters to bus drivers to kids on skateboards. They had been messed with, all their lives, and finally would tolerate no more.

What I've seen occurring quite often, among the pairs or groups of older women I see nattering loudly behind charity shop counters, on the bus, in markets or coffee queues is a kind of jostling, a bursting forth of need: to be seen, to be heard. To take up *space*.

At a cafe, a friend and I furtively watch four women who look to be aged between 70 and 80—lively, fashionable, middle-class feminists at play. They must be old friends, because normal rules of politeness appear to have gone out the window. They interrupt each other the instant they grow bored. One snatches a menu from another's hands. Another bellows at her friend to chew with her mouth closed, for God's sake! On one hand, I'm repelled by all this, but another part of me is riveted by the unashamed display of the secret self—that self we all have somewhere beneath our layers of approval-seeking and ambition and, yes, love and compassion. The secret self lies at our deepest core, and is closest to our infant self.

It's the self that wants to explode into tantrums when our desires are thwarted, that wants love—all of it, greedily, now.

We watch the women bickering, barking orders at each other, at the waitress. 'We have to make sure we don't end up doing this!' I hiss to my friend. But she's loving it. Not taking her eyes off them, she shakes her head slowly and says, 'I'm not making any promises.'

§

One thing Margaret Atwood has, that Helen Garner and Eimear McBride and Elizabeth Strout and the Magic Pudding have—and I hope I have—is laughter. Anger, surely, is ameliorated, made bearable, transformed by laughter. But into what? Impotence? Is that why women are both so angry and so helpless? (I just crossed 'helpless' out. You can't say women are *helpless*. We're not helpless! You'll get in trouble!)

Whatever it was that happened to the hesitant older woman, the self-declared angry woman, to Noor and all the women in all the wars, has obliterated the space for lightness inside a person, for laughter's redemption. And it's only luck that separates those who can laugh from those who can't.

Strout and Garner and the rest have something else, though, too: art. It's a home to go to, a place to take the shame and the rage and the confusion and the fear and lay it down, all of it, and stare it in the face. And in this space, we can wrangle it, conquer it, shape it into something transcendent or powerful, something funny, something beautiful.

Where do normal people take these feelings? What do they do with them?

§

There's a reckoning taking place now, we're told. Female anger is at last finding its mark and its moment. I hope this is my primitive anger-shame speaking, or jadedness, or simple weariness—but I can't trust it. The speed of the Me Too avalanche, its force, felt too dangerous. It felt like a runaway train that was going to crash off the rails, and soon. My own cheering at the sight of the bastards going down still feels too much like the delinquent ecstasy of a classroom run amok, and beneath this lurks the fear that when the frenzy's over, that will be that. And then we'll all cop it worse than before.

Is the woman who was too afraid to read my book rejoicing as she watches retribution raining down on a few affluent men across the Western world? Is this cathartic, curative, for her? I hope so. I hope the pain is flooding away from her spirit like a fast-running tide.

But I wonder.

§

On our living room wall is a strange sculpture by the artist Anita Johnson Larkin. It's long and thin, and takes up little space. At its base is an old sewing-machine foot and needle, stamping thick crimson stitches right into the wall. Your gaze follows this line of thread upwards, along a lusciously smooth, curving wooden spine, travelling through a series of tiny metal eyelets on prongs until it meets its source: a cotton reel fitted into a soft grey felted contraption. And then you see that the soft felted thing is a pistol, and the cotton reel its blood-red barrel, and the gun is pointing into the room, at you.

What's oddest, though, is that with its long narrow nose, its curved, slender body and the floating swatch of stitches at its tail, to me it has always most resembled a seahorse—delicate and sinister, dark and strong. Ethereal, creaturely, beautiful.

14

On Gods and Ghosts

•————————•

Catholicism, contradiction and creativity

One of my earliest memories is not a memory at all but a sensation, perhaps a kind of hunger: it is the taste of the wooden pew in the small church in which I spent every Sunday morning of my life from birth until high school. The ledge of the pew, where prayer books and hymnals and rosary beads rested, was just about shoulder height for a toddler wobbling to stand, so it was only natural to reach out and grasp hold of the ledge, put my mouth to its sweet, vinegary, golden wood, and suck.

§

Some experiences in life are so fundamental, wrote Norman Mailer in *The Spooky Art*, that he would characterise them as 'crystals'. Provided you never write directly about these experiences that carry deep and concentrated meaning, he claimed, by 'send[ing] a ray of your imagination through the latticework in one direction or another', the crystals might remain a precious, inexhaustible source for your art. It's impossible to refer to Mailer's book, of course, without acknowledging its passages of cringeworthy misogynistic posturing. But one of the things growing up Catholic taught me is that I can hold two opposing views in my head at once—and he's on to something with his crystals. I think they might be related to Uta Hagen's 'inner objects' that I've detailed elsewhere, those hidden essences of personal experience which, as long as they remain unspoken, can be useful sources of and stimuli for the artist's craft.

A constantly repeated question for every writer trying to make a work of art is: what else? And then, *what else?* What more is there beyond this moment of existence in the solid, material world to be discovered and then revealed? Another question might be about *where* that 'else', the longed-for missing knowledge, springs from in an artist's consciousness. I wonder if the original yearning—to name and articulate what cannot yet be said—is born in our wordless infancy, the pre-verbal space in a writer's experience, which in my case was so defined by those weekly hours in a country town church.

Each of my novels has drawn on my life's sense memories in hundreds of ways, large and small, but I've never properly considered the possibility that my religious upbringing might have formed a wellspring for my work. I don't know why it's not occurred to me before, but it now seems obvious you can't spend every Sunday morning of your life for eighteen years in the strange dusky space of a Catholic church without some of it rubbing off and going in—deep. If Catholicism formed my writing as definitively as it formed me, if it is one of my potent inner objects, my crystals, what might be the refractive glints coming off it?

Whatever they are, they were certainly undreamed of by Sister Fabian, swathed in her vast habit of winter black or summer white, clutching her cane. Or by Father Coffey spluttering Irishly from the pulpit (as small children we stared intently as he spoke—not listening, as he might have thought from our avid faces, but rather waiting for a thrilling glimpse of the hand on which half a finger was missing).

The first gift the weekly church service gave me was boredom— and its child, imagination. Compelled into motionless silence for a full hour every week while the language and imagery of the mass washed over us, we children were forced to draw upon our own minds for amusement. The effect on me, I'm convinced, was to bring into being an expansive and sovereign inner world. There was also something about the stillness and the absence of the parental gaze—ostensibly fixed on events at the altar—which allowed a feeling of supreme privacy. That small pocket of space between my seat, the kneeler and the back of the pew in front of me seemed an inviolate, secluded world. When I recall the church, it's not the altar and the priest I think of but the floorboards, the yellow wood grain of the pews, the green baize carpet and the musty shadows beneath the seats, the lozenges of stained-glass light falling across my knuckles clasped in 'prayer'. Of course everything about me was clearly visible to my parents or any other nearby adult the whole time, but it didn't *feel* that way: I felt luxuriously invisible. Paradoxically, then, it was this stern constraint of time and space each week in church that allowed the blossoming of an inner freedom.

The Bible itself offered other contradictory gifts to the unformed creative mind—especially if you were a girl. From where I sat, half listening, half daydreaming, the Bible was filled with angry fathers and their favoured or exiled sons. Sons and brothers were endlessly loved, sacrificed, envied, murdered, welcomed home, cast out; they were slavish or indolent, saviours or sinners. Family dramas were constant, violent, entirely male. There were no stories of sisters fighting or being saved. No baby girls were laid in baskets in the rushes. No daughters grew up to interpret pharaohs' dreams. Girl children appeared not to exist in ancient times. Women sometimes did, but only when they were wrong, and the cause of catastrophe. There was Eve, obviously. Lot's wife disobediently 'looked behind her' and turned into a pillar of salt. (I could never get over this: just for *looking*? And what *was* a pillar of salt?) Some names became midday-movie emblems of sexy evil-doing: Delilah, Salome. Other nameless women were always being stoned to death for adultery, or somehow punished for not having the right number of children (well, sons). The only women with any clear identity at all seemed to be the Virgin Mary and Mary Magdalene, but they were both infatuated with Jesus and spent their lives doing as he told them.

It wasn't just in the pages of the Bible that girls were invisible or boring. Stories of the saints, too, relied upon female self-denial and martyrdom. Girl saints especially were rewarded for meekness, piety and submission. To this day, I wonder what was going through Sister Fabian's mind when she waxed lyrical to a classroom full of eleven-year-old girls about St Maria Goretti, stabbed to death at age eleven for 'refusing to sin'. Sister Fabian declined to name the sin, so we knew it meant something obscure and shameful: sex. Maria was canonised, however, not just for resisting rape and violent death but, most importantly, for *forgiving* her murderer as she died.

The nuns I observed at school were all-powerful—until a priest arrived to visit. Then, even the rage-filled ones seemed both flattered by and in awe of the priestly male presence, transforming themselves into his ready servants. I don't know how old I was when I absorbed the knowledge of a nun's vows—poverty, chastity, obedience; defined by everything they couldn't have and nothing they could—but unlike other girls at school, never for one second did I dread the tap on the shoulder from God that would constitute the 'calling' to join up. Something resolute in me absolutely knew I would never give away so much for God.

In my teens, I heard a priest claim from the pulpit that feminism was 'evil'. He actually said that. How many other girls in the congregation flicked the last vestige of belief from themselves along with the droplets of holy water from their fingers that day?

I'd been absorbing the message from birth, really: if I didn't hate myself for being a girl, God had no interest in me. As I grew older, the occasional sad groovy priest or teacher would try out some feeble linguistic contortion about 'special' roles for women—not equal but 'chosen', 'valued', blah blah blah. All I felt for these people was embarrassment.

So. After all this, stupefied by boredom and increasingly outraged by double standards and hypocrisy, how can it be that at the same time, on some other plane, I was also nurtured and secretly enthralled by the Bible, the mass, the stories of the saints? I loved the lushness, the supernatural weirdness of the visions and miracles. I loved the dream-world reality in which a man could walk on water, where bushes could burst into flame but not incinerate, where oceans could part, bread fall from heaven. I loved the visceral, righteous dramas of betrayal and punishment and secrets, of lonely vigils in midnight gardens, of blood money paid in silver, the appearance and disappearance of foretelling angels, resurrections from the dead. I even loved the violence—the arrows and stones and knives and gore, the robes soaked in blood and vinegar, iron nails driven into flesh and thorns into scalp.

The ritual of the mass itself was an almost bodily lesson in narrative, structured in tension and release—the long stretches of monotony punctuated with bursts of movement where we, the slumped observers, were roused into action: the passing of the collection plate; the 'peace-be-with-you's, when you turned in your seat from the authority of the priest to focus on each other, where you might be called upon to speak to a stranger, where a bolder congregant might even *extend a hand*. And then—for long years the only point of interest—there was the opportunity for curious, detailed inspection of your fellow parishioners (and their fashion choices) as they stood in line for communion.

Inside the church itself, of course, there was the irresistible spectacle of excess: the brocade in gold and purple and forest green, the white marble, red carpet; the golden chalices and cups and little bowls, the candlelight and glowing flowers. I loved the transformation of annoying or faceless boys from school into languid holy creatures in flowing red robes and white ruffs, lying in dreamy reverie across the shallow stairs to the altar, occasionally ringing a bell or two. There was also a delicious, soaking cadence to the language of the Bible, with its repetitions and rhythms, its rocking two-by-twos and forty-days-and-forty-nights, its seven years of good luck and seven of bad, and there was a mystical potency in the symbols of apple and serpent and loaves and fishes, every mundane object rich with the possibility of another life, carrying layers of hidden meaning purely by existing.

Once, when quite young, I for some reason accompanied the child of another family to her Protestant Sunday school and found myself appalled. We sat on plastic chairs in a small meeting room bare of any sacred bling, and from a flimsy pamphlet were offered a dull, sweet children's story about lambs and being good. The adults in charge were creepily ingratiating, commanding no authority whatsoever. There was no gold, no robes, no violence or mystery. No otherworldliness or grandeur. There might have been biscuits, from a packet. I never went back.

I 'left' the Church around the time I finished school, by which I mean I stopped going to mass. I don't know if I'd ever actually believed in God, even in my most 'spiritual' moments, but for me that question was now settled: I was an atheist.

But in another way, nothing was settled. I could reject it all I liked, but it was too late to matter: I was awake to what was unseen, to the ghostly, the imaginative spirit. To sacrifice, to injustice. Catholicism had got into my bones as surely as the cold Monaro air filled my lungs, and despite almost never setting foot in a church again, I couldn't just will it away.

Artists have often derived enrichment from a religious sensibility. Some atheist writer friends of mine are compelled by the complexity of theology, or irresistibly drawn to the naked power manoeuvrings in Church hierarchy, or fascinated by the high camp of Catholic spectacle. But few writers are publicly candid about their faith in any kind of god—and those few must surely know it makes people suspicious. The courage it takes a writer to openly admit to spiritual belief shouldn't be underestimated. I once ran a writing retreat where, on the first evening, one of the participants broke into tears of genuine terror. She had something to confess, she said: she was a Christian. Her visceral fear of her fellow writers' judgement was awful to behold. I hope it was swiftly resolved that night—nobody appeared to care, whatever their private views may have been—but she was right to be afraid. In another group she might have been patronised, quietly frozen out, openly challenged or ridiculed.

As a species, Western writers are quick to show respect for Indigenous spiritual beliefs, for Islam or Judaism, Hinduism or Buddhism, but Christianity is a no-go zone. We all know why: even if you limit yourself to the Catholic Church's contemporary crimes of attitude or action—the homophobia, the racism, the misogyny, the remorseless abuse and hypocrisy—once you start writing them down, it's impossible to know where to stop.

Earlier, I mentioned holding two opposing ideas at once. It's a necessary capability, in order to accept that the practical Catholicism of my upbringing formed the sturdy basis of all I've learned about justice—protecting the vulnerable, standing up to oppression, sharing your wealth, telling the truth, owning your mistakes—while the same institution was simultaneously responsible for the most reprehensible cruelty, violence and abuses of children and of power. That some Catholic priests were sexually assaulting children without compunction at the same time some Catholic nuns were the only people prepared to touch our first AIDS patients is a contradiction impossible to reconcile. That the Church still employs elaborate financial and legal tactics to avoid compensating abuse victims while principled nuns like Patricia Fox and Veronica Openibo call out dictators and abusers is likewise impossible to reconcile. And the self-serving petty tyrants I observed as a young person could not be more dissimilar to the two priests, men of extraordinary compassion, intelligence and humility, I've come to know by chance as an adult.

These impossibilities, these contradictions, are endless. To a writer, they are interesting.

Not long ago I began a new novel. Its characters will include a small group of contemporary Catholic nuns. When I realised I wanted to write about this, I began buying books about Catholicism and women religious, and stacking them on my research reading shelf. I set about bookmarking articles on theology and religion, and subscribing to progressive Catholic publications like *Commonweal* and *The Tablet*. It dawned on me gradually that my failure to read these with any enthusiasm meant something more than laziness. It turns out it's not actually religion that interests me, creatively speaking. I realised I have little interest in theology or religious faith or even, I suppose, in God. The mark Catholicism left on me wasn't intellectual but bodily, instinctual and spooky; not so much godly as ghostly. I came to understand that my fascination with women religious—nuns—might be less about their spirituality and more about the decision to separate themselves from the rest of us. I'm interested in the kind of questions I can't ask: What are your dreams about? Who do you love? Why do you stay? What are your private joys, your unspeakable sorrows?

I'm interested, too, in the contrast between the kind of nun who does practical, radical and political 'good works' in the wider world—standing up to Trump or Duterte, or establishing climate solutions investment funds, or fighting for asylum seekers' rights— and the kind for whom *retreat* from the world of politics and action is the point. For this sort of woman, I wondered, might not the Catholic patriarchy be a means to unhook herself from the capitalist one? Despite the Church's views on women, it's not difficult for me to recognise the appeal of such a choice; to seek freedom in restraint and stillness rather than what's offered by the market economy with its own flourishing hatreds—not just of women, but of nature itself. This kind of woman might choose Catholicism over capitalism for her own ends, not anyone else's, even God's.

Some years ago I interviewed the art historian and writer Janine Burke, also raised Catholic. She articulated her own struggle with a church that had banished her from convent school for her sceptical questions and precocious reading: 'The interesting thing about Catholicism is that it awakens you spiritually to mystical, ecstatic states—and then the system just *crushes* you, it's brutal. So you end up . . . loathing the Catholic Church, but having had these extraordinary spiritual experiences.' For Burke, art filled the void.

I, too, turned to art, attracted by its yearning towards meaning, its unfazed acceptance of profound contradictions and connections that don't 'make sense', or which abandon logic altogether. It's the possibility of eventual transformation—transubstantiation?—of all this into some new clarity or revelation that's exciting.

But maybe the most powerful gift my religious upbringing gave me was my ambivalence towards it, and the resulting ability to dwell in a place of tension and discomfort that will never be eased. The constant movement between opposing states—between my desire for mystery and for knowledge, for communal duty and individual freedom, for belief and scepticism, the spiritual and material worlds, extravagance and humility, between political action and contemplative withdrawal—is the state of being an artist. This is what art does, this is where it lives: in the uncomfortable, often lonely space between one certainty and another.

It's obvious that you don't have to be Catholic, or any other religion, to understand this. Part of me thinks all true artists have an apprehension of the holy, whether they call it that or not. By 'holiness', I mean living with the sense that redemptive meaning shimmers somewhere beyond our reach, in a reality possible just outside our own. It's gods or ghosts who are in possession of the mighty stuff of art, and we have to wrestle them for it. We only ever glimpse it fleetingly, but we long for it nonetheless.

I think back to that child sitting in her dreamy private space between the church pews, the rhythms of ancient words about good and evil falling over her with the coloured, dusky light, and I know that's where I first felt the hunger, the 'art instinct': the understanding that something big was out there, that I would almost certainly never touch it, but that reaching for it was the point of being alive.

15

Between a Wolf and a Dog

Georgia Blain's final work

There's an unsettling moment in Georgia Blain's last novel when a man mourning his young daughter's death writes a letter to the self he was before the tragedy. It's part of his therapy, a scene that in more sentimental authorial hands might offer consolation, redemption. Not here. '*Dear Chris*,' he writes. '*You were such an ignorant idiot. And then you lost everything. I can't bear to look back on you.*'

'He was blessed with an ordinary life,' he says contemptuously of his former self. 'And he didn't even know.'

It's just one of many depth charges in *Between a Wolf and a Dog*, a novel of devastating clarity that traverses Blain's familiar terrain:

the ordinary sadnesses in families; betrayal and forgiveness; the small, priceless beauties of daily life that we allow to slip unnoticed through our fingers.

Between a Wolf and a Dog was Blain's seventh book for adults, released at the same time as *Special*, her sci-fi novel for young adults. While the timing might have been unusual, for her this level of productivity was unremarkable. But the notion of time took on a wrenching new urgency for Blain, 51, when shortly before the novel's publication she was diagnosed with incurable brain cancer. With aggressive treatment, she could expect to live another five years; without it, the tumour would return in months.

Her novel's title comes from a French expression, *L'heure entre chien et loup*: the hour between dog and wolf. It refers to the twilight time when falling darkness makes clear vision impossible; dogs might be mistaken for wolves, friends for foes.

The book had a long gestation. Blain wrote it several years before publication but set it aside while she helped her mother, renowned writer and journalist Anne Deveson, cope with her shattering diagnosis of Alzheimer's disease. Deveson could no longer live independently, so Blain and her family were left with the plaited sorrows of grieving, caring, house-clearing. As her mother's situation at home became untenable, Blain had begun editing the novel for publication.

Then came her own seizure, immediate surgery, the impossible prognosis.

Still in shock, Blain returned to work on the book days after her surgery, partly to start rehabilitating her facility with words. The tumour was right on her brain's language centre. Speech was affected; immediate and vigorous word use was essential.

As if these obstacles were not enough, she also faced a surreal irony in her work. As the novel opens, a central character, Hilary—a vibrant 70-year-old filmmaker, mother of therapist Esther and failed songwriter April—reveals to the reader but not her children that she has cancer, and that it has spread to her brain. Hilary is contemplating whether to end her own life before the disease does.

I spoke to Blain as her book was released into the world.

'When I went back to the copy edits I thought, "Oh God, am I going to feel differently about this book, now that I'm in Hilary's shoes?",' she told me as we drank herbal tea in her Marrickville living room, looking out over the serene green lawn where she had her seizure that dreadful day.

'The good thing was I didn't feel differently about the novel, but nor did I feel the same way the character does about her situation. I don't need to consider the choice that Hilary faces. For one thing, I'm in a different phase of life; I'm younger than she is. I have a partner and a daughter. I want to hang on to every chance I have to get myself a little bit more time.'

Time and its healing capacity—or not—is a central concern of *Between a Wolf and a Dog*. A betrayal between sisters, the ache of professional and personal failure, the commonplace yet genuine pain of the walking wounded who limp through Esther's therapist's office, are sensitively explored in Blain's spare, resolute prose.

Grief at sibling conflict and loss was a recurring theme of her work; it emerged again in both new novels. One of her two brothers, Jonathan, had schizophrenia as a teenager and his terrifying psychotic episodes and subsequent suicide are detailed in their mother's 1998 memoir, *Tell Me I'm Here*. Blain used to feel ashamed that her writing kept revealing a preoccupation with this wound.

> I was embarrassed about it—there was that male sort of notion that you had to write completely outside yourself, and you should be demonstrating a breadth of skill. But I'm not that kind of writer. And I'm not embarrassed anymore because many writers I love—like Alice Munro and Richard Ford, for example—write into the same material over and over. And what you write in your twenties is very different from how you interpret things when you're 50. You have quite a different angle on the same concerns.

Another recurring theme is the gap between one's political values and personal behaviour. The ethical ground of *Between a Wolf and a Dog* shifts when Lawrence, Hilary's pollster son-in-law, begins tweaking party polling results before releasing them to the media—just a little massaging of figures, in a subversive protest against the privileging of mob opinion over expert knowledge. Lawrence sees his work as 'the horrifying conclusion of democracy . . . everyone had the chance to speak. Worse still, the dross of it was being listened to; extracts of sludge were being drawn out, held up as truth.'

Blain's interest in this grew over twenty years of part-time work alongside a Fairfax Nielsen pollster colleague. Did she think this fakery of figures really happened?

No, not necessarily. But certainly pollsters push angles in their questions, and can shape the questions to focus on particular issues at the expense of others. You can keep pushing questions about the instability of a government, for example, so you create the story. And when you give the poll results to the media, you frame them in certain ways. You say, 'Look, the startling result here is this.' And of course journalists can unpack this, but they don't, always.

Blain's artistic gaze was unerring, her characters never idealised.

'I get slammed for having unlikable characters. My women are often ambivalent about parenthood, they're seen as stern and too reserved—but I never, ever think they're unlikable at *all*. I'm always completely flummoxed! I think, "Oh, I thought she was quite nice!" But there are two consistent criticisms: I talk too much about the privileged middle class, and my women aren't likable. It used to worry me,' she says, laughing, 'but now I couldn't give a rat's arse.'

Her ability to laugh during our conversation—she makes many black and very funny jokes—astounded me, as did her claim that in some ways she felt lucky.

'I don't want to sound Pollyanna-ish and say it's a good thing to have cancer. It's a fucking awful thing to have cancer. But as my surgeon told me when he delivered the bad news, I have a chance to reassess my life and how I spend my time now. And I feel lucky to have found love in my life, when many people don't.'

Too ill now from chemotherapy side effects to start a new book, Blain began a short monthly newspaper column about her cancer called 'The Unwanted Guest'. It's piercing reading, customarily unflinching, beautiful in its honesty and clarity.

'I can write, which is good, but I'm grasping the possibility now that I might be this sick until the day I die,' she said. 'When I plummet, I try to keep hold of the hope that this part is temporary.'

Near the end of *Between a Wolf and a Dog*, Hilary observes: 'All around her it is quiet and still. *It is that hour*, she thinks. Where day turns to night.'

That hour, that ambiguous space between light and dark, between embracing what's possible and falling into despair, was Blain's uneasy new home.

'There's a sort of stillness now, after the first flurry. Which is tricky. I have to ask how do I live, in the time I have left? I guess I've ended up writing about just this question. What are the things that genuinely make us happy? How do we measure those things? How do we work out what really matters, before the end?'

Georgia Blain died in December 2016, three days before she would have turned 52. In the last months of her life, Georgia wrote a final book, The Museum of Words: A memoir of language, writing, and mortality. *It was published posthumously in 2017.*

16

Useful, Pleasurable, Strange

•————————•

Growing old as an art form

A few years ago, a pretty young woman approached me in the lunchroom of the building where I began work on my novel, *The Weekend*.

'You're writing about ageing, aren't you?' she asked.

I was, I said, smiling.

She considered my 50-year-old face for a few long seconds before shuddering: 'I'm terrified of ageing.'

I burst out laughing.

But she's not alone. Looking down the tunnel to old age, it seems we're all afraid. But of what, exactly? How should we think about growing old?

§

At a dinner, I sat next to a darkly witty gerontologist. He was under no illusions about very old age—at one point in our conversation there came some pragmatic deliberation about the best way to kill yourself when the time came. But he was also keen to stamp on a few old-people clichés.

He told me of an elderly man brought to an appointment by his children. They were deeply concerned, wanting him assessed for dementia. His major symptom was falling in love with a sex worker, moving her into his house, giving her money and property. The doctor reluctantly put him through rounds of rigorous tests—and found absolutely nothing wrong with his cognition or psychology. He was sane, he was loved, he was happy. The doctor hooted with delight as he told me this story.

Later, he asked me: 'How many years of your life would you trade for a Booker Prize?'

'What?! None!' I replied. I was surprised at the vehemence and speed of my answer, and that I knew it to be absolutely true.

Then he asked, 'What if they were the years between 85 and 95?'

Hmmm.

§

My friend J reports on her mother, very slowly dying in a nursing home. She's in her late 90s, and so frail her heart has not the strength to push blood to the extremities of her body. Her hands and feet are bloodless, cold. Yet when she's wheeled into a patch of sunshine in the garden, she smiles with deep, sensual pleasure. 'How lovely this is,' she says with relish. Soaking up the warmth, the sound of the trees moving above her.

J's sister leaves a nursing home visit one day in bleak distress. 'I can't go in there anymore,' she says.

J agrees that it's very hard, but is curious. What especially prompted this today?

Her sister's expression is almost angry. 'It's that she just . . . lies there. She's so—' She searches for the word, then finds it. '*Useless.*'

Another friend's mother, also in her 90s, was taken to inspect a potential nursing home. Through a doorway she saw some residents in an exercise class.

'What's wrong with them?' she barked loudly.

'Nothing,' her daughter said. 'They're just . . . old.'

'Well,' said the mother viciously, 'they look *retarded.*'

A different woman, unwell at 79, needed aqua therapy at a rehab centre but refused to enter the pool. 'I'm not getting in that water. It's full of *disgusting old bodies.*'

Everyone in the pool was visibly younger than she.

A man in late middle age invited his 86-year-old father to live with him and his family. It hasn't worked out well. The son describes the sound of his father's walker creaking down the hall. 'I hate him,' he says.

Is this dread of the mirror so deeply rooted in all of us? Is it a biological imperative, to turn away as soon as we catch our reflection?

§

In 2015, a review in an Australian newspaper rebuked Edna O'Brien for her wild, chaotic and (I thought) stupendously adventurous novel, *The Little Red Chairs*. The reviewer's main point was not so much that the book was flawed, though it surely is, but that the cause of these flaws was the author's advanced age. What I read, between the faux-respectful lines, was an unprinted command to O'Brien: You're old. You're embarrassing yourself. Shut up.

O'Brien was 85 at the time. Her latest novel, *Girl*, about the Nigerian girls abducted by Boko Haram, was published when she was 89. She's still writing.

Not shutting up, then.

§

Our predictions for old age foresee an epoch of physical incapacity and psychic misery, in contrast with our vital, flourishing youth. But last night on my couch I spent five minutes scribbling down a list of the troubles that plagued me and those in my extended social circle—middle class, well educated, well resourced—before we turned 50.

Major depression. Anorexia and bulimia. A birth malformation necessitating fifteen years of agonisingly painful surgery and follow-up treatments. Panic attacks and agoraphobia. Kidney disease. Broken arms and legs. Chronic, intensifying lung disease. Bipolar disorder leading to job and relationship loss, financial disaster. Endometriosis. Crohn's disease and irritable bowel syndrome with frequent hospitalisation. Asthma, fatal. Asthma, chronic, multiple hospitalisations. Excruciating diverticulitis. Migraines and an inability to hold a job. Severe postnatal depression. HIV/AIDs, mostly fatal. Type 1 diabetes and complications. Juvenile arthritis with attendant chronic immobilising pain. Major paranoid psychosis, forced hospitalisation and trauma. Cardiac problems, multiple open-heart surgeries. Schizophrenia causing lifelong inability to work and extreme social isolation. Melanoma. Bowel cancer, fatal. Breast cancer, fatal and non-fatal. Brain cancer, fatal and non-fatal. Stevens-Johnson syndrome caused by medical malpractice. Stomach cancer, fatal. Strokes, locked-in syndrome, fatal. Severe addiction to illegal drugs, alcohol, prescription painkillers. Chronic and acute immobilising pain in spine, knee, neck, foot. Knee and shoulder surgery, severely limiting mobility. High blood pressure. Car accidents, frequently fatal. Farm accidents. Multiple sclerosis. Guillain-Barré syndrome. Suicide attempts. Suicide.

After five minutes I stopped scribbling. Excluding a couple of the cancers, almost all of these issues had first occurred before age 30; many have persisted into the fifth and sixth decades. Yet some cognitive dissonance allows us to perceive even long-term disorders in youth as somehow aberrant, manageable and far less horrifying than the potential 'degradations' of old age.

I recently saw a birthday card bearing the image of a haughtily elegant middle-aged woman in 1950s attire. The caption read: 'Honey, you couldn't pay me to be twenty.' I bought it immediately.

I was not a happy or a healthy young person. I had chronic asthma exacerbated by smoking; I was unfit; my diet was ordinary. 'Orphaned' by 29, I spent most of my 20s and 30s in grief. I was deeply anxious with little confidence, my fretful neediness causing relationship problems. For many of those years, I cried every week.

The day I turned 50, I felt a mysterious surge of what I could only think of as power. A deep optimism, energy and peacefulness took up space inside me. Give or take a few crises since, it hasn't really left. In my mid-50s, I'm physically and emotionally stronger, healthier, more calmly loved and loving, more productive, more organised, smarter, wealthier and exponentially happier than I ever was in my youth. In the past four years I've really cried about three times, on one occasion because a good friend died.

I mentioned my mid-life happiness at a public event once. A woman in the audience called out cheerfully, 'You think it's great when you're 50—wait till you're 70!'

There are global studies showing what's called 'the paradox of age', a U-curve revealing that from childhood onwards happiness declines, and then dramatically rises. We're most miserable in our 40s, but things pick up around 50; happiness at 90 far exceeds that at 18. This upswing is partly owing to life experience, but is also a direct result of getting older, say psychologists: 'The biological, cognitive and emotional changes of aging itself . . . result in better emotional regulation, greater equanimity and compassion, more comfort with ambiguity, deeper gratitude and a focus upon meaningful engagement in the present.'

Having published a novel about older women, I'm now seeing evidence of joyful, mischievous ageing everywhere I go. A woman at a book event tells me that, at 77, she'd resigned herself to a life that was winding down, finishing up. Instead, she says in astonishment, 'I can't stop the ideas coming. I just have ideas and ideas and ideas!' She motions with both hands outwards from her head, in a delighted gesture of pouring abundance. Her husband sits beside her, beaming.

Another day I overhear two women—perhaps they're 80— outside a cinema. One tells the other she's being badgered to visit her daughter, a long drive away in the country. She looks into the middle distance then says serenely, 'I think she wants me to go before I *lose my licence.*' The two women look at each other for a second, then burst into loud cackles. They gather their bags and stride into the movie house.

§

What am I afraid of, when I think about old age? I'd like to say nothing, but that would be untrue. Dementia, obviously. Relentless physical pain so bad it eclipses small pleasures. Being forced to live with people I dislike. Loss of autonomy. The kind of poverty that destroys autonomy. Unstinting boredom caused by an inability to read or hear.

I fear becoming a bitter, self-pitying person. Taking up genealogy. Boring other people to death with my 'wonderful stories'.

What am I not afraid of? Living alone. Being 'invisible'. The body's gradual decline, notwithstanding the above. Being dead.

It's possible I'm completely deluded. When these things befall me, I'll probably be petrified.

§

In 'Why we can't tell the truth about aging', an article in the *New Yorker*, Arthur Krystal sneers at the recent proliferation of 'feel-good' books about getting older. It's sheer trendiness to put a positive spin on growing old, Krystal grouches: the truth is, it sucks—please let's stop the lying.

He appears unconvinced by the U-curve.

But he has a point. It's true that alongside the horror and revulsion there has now emerged quite a bit of jolly crusading about the fabulousness of old age. Like Krystal, I too find irksome the anti-ageism books refusing to acknowledge the downsides, those calling for a special new language with which to 'celebrate' ageing. Ditto the sappy memes that pop up now and then on social media. (*Wrinkles are engraved smiles?* Jesus Christ.) Nor am I drawn to heart-warming movies in the genre that *New York Times* critic Neil Genzlinger calls Old People Behaving Hilariously. I cheer when Anjelica Huston sniffs her disdain for 'apologetically humble or humiliating' film roles, like one in 'an old-lady cheerleader movie'. I'm with you, Anjelica, I think. When I'm your age I want my work taken seriously, too. But then I read of a response from Jacki Weaver, who's in the old-lady cheerleader movie. When she read Huston's comments, Weaver says, 'I just laughed. And then I said, "Well, she can go fuck herself."'

I snort jubilantly into my coffee cup. Go, Jacki! I'm with you, too.

§

Palliative care nurses have told me people almost always die as they live. A person who has lived with acceptance and gratitude will die in gracious acceptance. One who's lived in bitterness and entitlement and anger will likely die in the same state. Suddenly it's blindingly obvious to me that ageing is the same; all our prior years are practice for the hard stuff of getting old. When I think of the old individuals I know who express delight and curiosity in ordinary daily life, a sense of purpose and appreciation, I realise that, give or take a few tragedies, they've always been this way. It's their default state. When I think of the unhappiest old people I know—victimised, spiteful, ungrateful for small pleasures, eternally dissatisfied and offended—I look back and see those traits governing their early and middle years too.

Note to self: Practise hard.

Question to self: When is it too late to change one's default state?

§

The *Good Weekend* magazine carries an account of life in a nursing home ('one of the good ones') by a perceptive retired journalist in his early 80s. He writes brilliantly, the by-line is a pseudonym and the article is gloomy stuff. One of the worst things he relates is enduring mealtimes with a fellow resident as she snatches and grasps, losing her manners, insulting the staff, and bullying a vulnerable fellow resident.

A week later, a letter appears in the *Good Weekend* from an 84-year-old retired pathologist. His experience of residential care, 'in an affluent Melbourne suburb', is much better. 'Ageing,' writes

Peter Thomson of Ivanhoe, 'is inevitable, inexorable and interesting. AAA rating for ageing: Anticipate, Adapt, Accept.'

Ageing is *interesting*! I keep this letter and think of it often. It might be the most uplifting set of instructions I've ever read.

It also points to something else that's scary: positive ageing takes money.

My partner and I talk about our Sydney mortgage. Unless suddenly showered with astonishing riches—unlikely—we'll have paid it off when he turns 78 and I'm 76. I think: We'll just move to the country. We'll just move into a bedsit. We'll just move. As if that will solve everything.

When I talk with other people in the arts about 'retirement plans', we all laugh grimly. One says hers is to poke out an eye with the car aerial and claim compensation. Another has his sights on a salubrious cardboard box on the median strip as a retirement villa. Nobody has any superannuation to speak of—when the average writer's income is $11,000 per year, where would it come from?

We'll all just keep working, we say gamely. We'll keep writing, painting, performing. How could we stop, anyway? We wouldn't want to stop. We talk about Matisse and his paper cut-outs, Edna O'Brien, Wallace Stegner. Adapting, accepting, but always making, always working.

None of us states the obvious: we're not Matisse, or O'Brien, or Stegner. No one talks about what will happen when nobody wants our work anymore.

§

In recent years, it's come to me that the point of all our living is to get ready to die. People laugh when I say this out loud. How morbid to think of death all the time! But I don't find it morbid. I find it stimulating, a purposeful exercise, considering how to live—to strive towards living—with that readiness inside us.

The Jungian psychologist James Hillman posits that the purpose of human ageing is to fulfil our true character, to become our essential selves. More radically, he suggests that ageing might be 'a transformation in beauty as much as in biology'. And then he asks a truly shocking question: Could ageing itself be conceived of as an art form?

If it can, then maybe artists can teach us to practise it. Push beyond your first ideas, they might say. Develop a tolerance for solitude, and for failure. Make your mark, defend it, then challenge it, overturn it.

Jerry Saltz: 'Don't think good or bad. Think useful, pleasurable, strange.'

Walt Whitman: 'I am large, I contain multitudes.'

Helen Frankenthaler: 'I'd rather risk an ugly surprise than rely on things I know I can do.'

Jasper Johns again: 'Take an object. Do something to it. Do something else to it.'

§

I've asked what we're really afraid of, looking ahead to old age. I think the deepest dread is of being reduced, simplified. We're afraid that, to paraphrase British psychologist and writer Susie Orbach, we'll be robbed of the richness of who we are, our complexity stripped away by forces beyond our control. This reduction is already happening with the cheerleaders on one side, the catastrophisers on the other. Ours is an all-or-nothing, black-and-white-thinking culture; we picture ourselves as either relentlessly active, plank posing and Camino walking and cycling into our 90s, or dribbling in a nursing-home chair, waiting for death.

But maybe we don't have to choose either extreme to dwell on. Maybe we can be Anjelica *and* Jacki; be large, contain multitudes. Perhaps, instead of capitulating to reduction, we can keep adding to our concept of how to age—turn our thinking about oldness into an art, and keep exploring it. Doing something to it, and doing something else.

17

The Rapture

●——————————●

Nature and the artist

When I was small, my mother would leave the newest baby in a pram in the garden to sleep, or to gaze up at the movement of the trees high above. I'm not sure how long she left us there for, or what she did inside the house while we lay in the cool air outside, blinking and staring, kicking our bare legs, snuffling quietly in the way new babies do. Perhaps she was sleeping herself, or reading, or more likely doing household chores without small children underfoot. At least one sibling would have been playing nearby. Family legend has it that our mother once came to retrieve me from the pram to find that my two-year-old big sister had fed me a little meal from the garden; apparently I lay there peacefully sucking on a mouthful of stones and twigs.

I can't possibly remember lying in that garden as a baby, but I feel that I do, parked on the grass in the giant old-fashioned pram, contented and contained, my senses free to roam and absorb everything around me: the smell of the pram's vinyl walls mixed in with the menthol scent of the large eucalypt gracing the front yard of our house. The sound of bees in the flowers, the falling, gulping calls of the currawongs. I can still see the hypnotic movement above me, the shifting black tracery of the eucalypt leaves against a white summer sky.

What goes through a baby's mind as she lies mesmerised in her pram, considering the shapes, colours, smells and sounds coming to her? Does she understand these sensations, this natural world, as separate from or part of herself? Does she create meaning from what she senses here, or does it all remain a strange, beautiful mystery?

I know this memory from the pram can't be accurate because by the time we lived in that house I was four years old. But perhaps the feeling of it is so strong because my whole childhood seemed to take place entirely outdoors: first in the various corners and secret caverns beneath shrubs and in the flowerbeds of our garden, and later in the bush reserve a few blocks from home, where we were allowed to wander for hours, even whole days, completely unsupervised.

We spent every summer holiday at the coast, camping by the beach for three weeks each January. Our days were filled with sandcastles, paddling, tooling around rockpools, building campfires and wandering in the surrounding bush. Barely clothed, brown as berries, hatless and free.

It's because of all this, I suppose, that I've felt at home in the natural world since birth. And as a writer I've always known, without understanding or questioning why, that my feelings for nature and my creative impulse are deeply connected.

There is one exception to this ease with the natural world: I've never been a water person. My blissful memories of the beach are always of the shore. Even those times we kids set off on adventures to the rock caves that would fill with rushing water as the tide came in, sand was always visible through the clear water. And even as the water rose and we waded chest high through the wash, my feet could always touch the bottom.

The odds were probably against an easy affinity with the ocean from the start, growing up as I did in an inland country town with English parents whose own feelings about the fierce Australian surf were ambivalent, at best. There were obligatory swimming lessons at the local pool, of course, and our dad erected a hot blue plastic above-ground pool in our backyard every summer. But I never learned to love the sea.

When I was three, my pregnant mother took my five-year-old sister, my twelve-month-old brother and me by ship to Britain, to meet our grandparents. I can't imagine now how stressful it must have been for her to make this journey alone—they couldn't afford the fare for Dad to go too—and I recall very little about the several weeks we were at sea. Could we kids even have seen the ocean around us? Surely we were too small to peer over any railings.

But I must have absorbed some of my mother's apprehension about this trip. I have only two distinct memories of the weeks on board. First, of shuffling along in a little procession of child mermaids, wearing a green crepe-paper costume my mother somehow put together for a fancy-dress party. My older sister won the costume contest: she was the old woman who lived in the shoe with too many children, pushing a pram filled with all of our dolls and our baby brother.

My other memory is more disturbing. One day, an enormous gathering took place on an upper deck in the blinding sunlight, beside the giant swimming pool. As hordes of adult strangers crushed in, we kids pressed nervously against our mother. Then, on some sudden invisible signal, every hitherto-sensible grown-up in the place began screaming and bellowing, many violently shoving at one another until they plunged, fully clothed, into the pool. I recall *ice cream* being flung about. And in this horrifying pandemonium, the air filled with the sound of frenzied adult laughter.

Much later I learned of the traditional 'crossing the line' celebrations that take place as ships traverse the equator. But at three years old, cleaved rigid with fear to my mother's leg, all I knew was that the orderly world was collapsing. Water—everywhere outside the ship, and now inside it—was associated with unstoppable chaos, and terror. (I've only just now wondered about a connection between that journey on the ship and the recurring childhood nightmare I mentioned in an earlier chapter, in which 'drowning', albeit in space rather than water, was the great fear.)

As the summers passed, we learned of the more ordinary dangers of the sea. Another family camped at the same beach we did every year. We didn't really associate with them, these kids who roared into the surf, invincible, conquering. They were big and rough and loud, like the ocean itself. Proper Australian children, they were absolutely fearless in the water. One day, three of them were caught in a rip as they clung to the great black inner tube of a tractor tyre, and were swept out to sea. I remember all the adults in the campground going quiet, staring and staring towards the horizon as the little black smudge swept further out, and further still. Eventually the children were rescued by a fishing boat and brought home again, triumphant.

My husband was once caught in a rip as a child with his brother and sisters, dragged out just like that, but minus the flotation device. At one point, he says, knowing they'd soon drown, the children all began to laugh. Laughing and laughing, hysteria sweeping them out with the current. Eventually the rip curled, changed direction and delivered them, exhausted, back on the shore. Their parents, dozing on the sand, hadn't even noticed they were gone.

Back home in our town, as we grew older and reached high school, the local pool was abandoned for the river: more private, wilder, more dangerous. The brown water of the Murrumbidgee covered hidden horrors: slimy riverweed, sharp sticks, snakes. Beneath the surface was an old sunken bridge, with its invisible iron bolts and jagged edges waiting to gash your thigh, or yank a swimsuit strap from your shoulder.

The river was where the cool kids smoked and drank beer, and wrestled with one another in the water and out of it. Where hotted-up cars revved and threatened. I smoked my first cigarette there in the bushes—a Craven A Filter stolen from my father's packet. I had my first drink at the river, too, and my first kiss, in the summer dark. Wet bathers, wet hair and the dark undertow of desire and trespass now joined the other fears awash in my subconscious. To have a body was awful, exhilarating, menacing. And there was water once again, now with its sinister threat of a new kind of drowning.

The undertow, my dream, the tide; the simultaneous yearning for and dread of being swept away.

Jung said the sea represents the unconscious, after all.

§

Yesterday I walked up to the flannel flowers again.

For a couple of years now I've lived part-time away from the city in a house near the sea, surrounded by bush. There's a path behind our

213

house up into the national park, and in spring the flannel flowers come out. This past year, as if in compensation for the pandemic's terrors and griefs, the flowers have burst forth with shocking abundance.

As you walk the path, your heart lifts at the first sighting. The flowers prefer stony, exposed ground, appearing in small clutches of one or two small, spindly plants, but their chalky whiteness glows brightly against the grey-green of the surrounding bush.

Then, rounding a bend, you see whole clumps of them lining the path, and your breath catches. Then there's a flare in the corner of your vision, and you turn and can't help but cry out at the graceful stony terraces laid out beneath the angophoras, *covered* in flowers. The bush gleams, frothy with white.

All I can think of is Wordsworth. 'When all at once I saw a crowd . . .'—he felt this same gasp, this same stunned joy.

§

Artists and writers have always turned to nature for solace, inspiration and refreshment. Several times in my life, in some natural place, I've experienced what at another point in history might have been deemed a kind of ecstatic religious swoon. These occurrences are not the same as the transports I've had quite often, as on my flannel-flower walk, but something deeper, more mysterious, quite bodily and always strongly connected with the creative work I've been engaged in at the time.

Rapture is not too strong a word for these moments. Even if I've been with others at the time, it hasn't felt that way, for the feeling was so private and inexpressible. I've felt it walking through a shady glade in a Lisbon botanical garden, and on seeing the enormous head of a humpback whale corkscrew silently up from the water near our tourist boat. I've felt it walking in the softly falling snow in a Tasmanian national park, and even when squatting to pee in the dry grass outside a rudimentary cabin in the bush where I once spent a week working on a book.

Each of these times the rapture has descended unexpectedly and with such intensity it's felt like a gift from some other place, somewhere larger and older and beyond human perception or time. It's at once a strongly physical feeling and an ethereal one, as if I've entered some unearthly state.

Artists have no special claim on the rhapsodic influence of nature, and I know that people with all kinds of different interests and pursuits and life experiences reading this will recognise their own moments of something resembling this state. But because I'm a writer, I do feel in this state of being an undeniable connection to my work, for it mirrors a condition I associate with the deepest creative absorption. Part of it is a sense of my edges blurring; a feeling I've had in meditation occasionally, but quite often when I'm thoroughly inhabiting the imagined world of a book. The delineation between myself and the world around me softens and dissolves. It's a transcendent, mystical experience.

But it's not that mystical. We know from study after study that cognition and creativity are enhanced by immersion in the natural world. It's no accident that artists' colonies like Bundanon and Varuna in Australia—and their international counterparts at Yaddo and MacDowell in the United States, the Tyrone Guthrie Centre in Ireland's Annaghmakerrig, the Bellagio Center on the shores of northern Italy's Lake Como, among many others—are established in serene natural surroundings.

The creativity researcher Mihaly Csikszentmihalyi is one of those who has written about the connection between creative breakthroughs and natural beauty. A stunning view is not a silver bullet, he says, but, nevertheless, his research has shown that 'when persons with prepared minds find themselves in beautiful settings, they are more likely to find new connections among ideas, and new perspectives'.

It was during a week I once spent at the coast, writing intensely and walking daily on the beach or in the bush in the same part of the country where I now spend so much time, that I had the most profound experience of my creative life. I now know it met Csikszentmihalyi's criteria for 'the flow experience'—for me, a rare and miraculous state.

This flow state lasted a few hours. I was nearing the end of a long and arduous rewrite of a troublesome novel, and I was weary.

I felt too close to the book to see what I had done, that period where one is in danger of causing more damage to a work that already feels disjointed and clunky. But on this particular afternoon as I laboured away, a sense of total ease and loose, magical command descended upon me, seemingly from nowhere. The whole book, previously so misshapen and lumpen, now appeared absolutely whole and clear and present in my mind, so much so that it felt I was actually inside it, moving swiftly through the entire work. I knew exactly what to do and where and how to do it. I could lift sections and shift them to precisely the right place elsewhere in the novel, deepening and repairing, using solutions and ideas that had never come to me in all the years I'd struggled with the book. All of this was infused with an utterly natural sense of conviction and a serene euphoria.

When I staggered away from the desk that day, I knew something astonishing had taken place, an almost spiritual transcendence. I'm certain it was born of the long end-stage of that book's gestation—my preparedness of mind, as Csikszentmihalyi says—but only because it was combined with my deep immersion in the natural world that week, and the living harmony of my surroundings.

It has never—alas—happened again in that way, but I have been visited by less-ecstatic versions of that absorption and confidence. And though I don't understand it, I fervently believe in the positive influence of nature on the creative mind.

Perhaps it's to do with a shift in scale and perspective, with feeling helpfully insignificant in the face of greatness when we look at the vast sea or a ridgeline of olive-green bush. Perhaps it's to do with the ancient solidity of stone beneath our feet, and the understanding that our petty concerns are as nothing in the earth's grand timeline. I don't know what it is, and in some important way I don't want to know. I feel superstitious about it, fearing that if I discover too much about why and when it happens, I might chase away the awe.

§

Since I've been spending so much time in this house between the bush and the sea, something has slowly begun to change in me. I'm calmer, personally and creatively. In the warmer months I've grown used to swimming not once or twice in the season, but once or twice a day. For the first time in my life I own more than one swimsuit, and the clothesline is always draped with wet bathers and a beach towel. It's silly, but somehow I feel at last a belonging to the place, this country, because of the sea. And that old nightmare, with its dread of the unknown deep, seems so distant now it could have been dreamed by someone else.

I wrote this new feeling for the ocean into the ending of my novel *The Weekend*. Three friends stand in the sea together at dawn, each having faced a devastating loss of certainty through the course of the book. One, Adele, is a good swimmer, the others more reluctant and afraid.

She had lost, she felt, a great deal. But here in the water her frightened friends were gripping her hands. Holding on to Adele for dear life. The swell grew, larger and larger. Jude and Wendy feared its approach, feared the great unrolling wall of water, but Adele kept firm hold of their hands, and called, 'Don't worry. Go under when I tell you.' She made them wait, the strong instrument of her body persuading, and she counted and said, *now*.

And each of the three let go, plunged down and felt herself carried, lifted up in the great sweep of the water's force, and then—astonishingly gently—set down on her feet again. They breathed and wiped their eyes, reached for each other again, waited for the next wave.

§

One recent summer morning, as I walked home alone from a swim, a thought arrived like clear cold water: *This is the happiest moment of my life.* It had been a rough year in many ways; the future was uncertain. Nevertheless, I was happy. I loved my partner, and all our close people were healthy. It was to do with my work, too; I'd finished a book, felt I'd given it my all, and I had the sense of completion and quiet pride that comes at such a time. But more than all that, it was to do with the sea, with taking the sound of the ocean into sleep. The great stretch of water, with its endless sweep and drag, now felt like connectedness: this chill water glazing my body was miraculously joined to every other ocean and sea and bay on the planet. And now the idea of being a tiny speck, carried and lifted, was restful and consoling. I have found in the ocean some deep release, a rinsed acceptance of how things are. Maybe I've surrendered to the great unconscious, each cold submersion gradually reconciling me to the scattered parts of my hidden self, without strain or resistance.

This morning I stepped into the cold waves beneath a smoky bushfire sky. The breath whooshed out of me, reminding me that I'm more than just neuroses and thoughts.

Here in the sea I'm at once all body, and no body at all. It's no surprise that baptism involves such immersion. The salt water is a blissful shock, of luck and the life force.

I'm alive, I'm free. I've exhaled.

AUTHOR'S NOTE

●————————————————●

Early versions of most chapters in this book have appeared in other publications, although all have since been revised, edited or rewritten.

'Fertile Ground' first appeared in *The Age* and the *Sydney Morning Herald* in April 2020. A version of 'The Getting of Wisdom' first appeared in the *Sydney Morning Herald* in 2018. 'The Grumpy Struggle' emerged from a keynote address to the Australasian Asscociation of Writing Programs in 2017. An early version of what became 'Unconscious Bias' was published in *Good Weekend* magazine in 2012. 'An Element of Lightness' appeared in an early version under a different title in *The Guardian* in 2018. *The Guardian* also first published 'Afraid of the Dark' (2017) and 'On Gods and Ghosts' (2020) under different titles. 'Strange Bedfellows' began life as a speech delivered at the Art Gallery of New South Wales during the exhibition of The Lady and the Unicorn tapestries in 2018. The *Sydney Review of Books* published early versions of 'Letting In the Light' (2014) and 'Reading Isn't Shopping' (2018). Versions of 'Cat and Baby' (2020) and 'Take an Object' (2016) were first published under other titles by *Literary Hub*. 'The Paint Itself' borrows several paragraphs from my introduction to *The Best Australian Stories 2016*, published by Black Inc. A version of 'The Outside Voice' first appeared under the title 'In Praise of Feral Women' in Bri Lee's quarterly periodical *Hot Chicks with Big Brains*. *Between a Wolf and a Dog* was first published as a portrait of Georgia Blain by the *Sydney Morning Herald* in 2016. 'Useful, Pleasurable, Strange' first appeared under a different title in *Griffith Review* in 2020. And an early version of 'The Rapture' appeared in *Good Weekend* magazine in 2019.

REFERENCES

●━━━━━━━━━●

1. FERTILE GROUND

p. 6   'I am constantly meeting ladies'
        Patrick White. Letter to James Stern, March 1966. *Patrick White: Letters*. Edited by David Marr, Random House Australia, Sydney, 1996.

p. 6   '"Just go up there and write it!"'
        Nicholson Baker. *The Anthologist*. Simon & Schuster, London, 2009.

p. 7   'the most creative mood state'
        Matthijs Baas, Carsten K.W. De Dreu and Bernard A. Nijstad. 'A meta-analysis of 25 years of mood-creativity research: Hedonic tone, activation, or regulatory focus?' *Psychological Bulletin*, vol. 134, no. 6, 2008.

p. 9   'Be regular and orderly in your life'
        Gustave Flaubert. Various translations of 'Be settled in your life and as ordinary as the bourgeois, in order to be fierce

and original in your works'. Letter from Gustave Flaubert
to Gertrude Tennant, 25 December 1876.

p. 9   'I will get up every morning no later than eight'
      Susan Sontag. *As Consciousness is Harnessed to Flesh: Journals
      and notebooks 1964–1980*. Edited by David Rieff.
      Picador, New York, 2012.

2. THE GETTING OF WISDOM

p. 13   'looking for trouble'
      'Philip Roth: The art of fiction no. 84'. Interview by
      Hermione Lee. *Paris Review*, issue 93, 1984.

p. 15   'Competence is the enemy of art'
      Michelle de Kretser. *The Lost Dog*. Allen & Unwin, Sydney,
      2007.

3. THE GRUMPY STRUGGLE, DESPAIR AND THE LUMINOUS SOLUTION

p. 19   'Once I'm working'
      'Janet Burroway talks about writing lives'. *CMOS Shop Talk.
      The Chicago Manual of Style*, 4 April 2014.

p. 20   'scrub bashing'
      Jason Steger. 'It's fiction and that's a fact'. *The Age*, 29 March
      2008.

p. 21   'a difficulty is perceived or felt'
      John Dewey. *How We Think*. D.C. Heath, Boston, 1910.

REFERENCES

p. 22   'It is in fact the *discovery and creation*'
        J.W. Getzels and M. Csikszentmihalyi. *The Creative Vision:*
          A longitudinal study of problem finding in art. Wiley, New
          York, 1976.

p. 23   'multiple cycles of problem-solving activities are required'
        M.D. Mumford and S.B. Gustafson. 'Creative thought:
          cognition and problem solving in a dynamic system'. *The*
          Creativity Research Handbook (vol. 2). Edited by Mark A.
          Runco. Hampton Press, New Jersey, 2012.

p. 24   'what matters most isn't there at all'
        'Philip Roth: The art of fiction no. 84'. Interview by
          Hermione Lee. *Paris Review*, issue 93, 1984.

p. 24   'I get a bit caught up'
        Lloyd Jones. Interview by Charlotte Wood. *The Writer's*
          Room. Allen & Unwin, Sydney, 2016.

p. 25   'the most interesting thing is to back yourself'
        Chuck Close. Interview by Joe Fig. *Inside the Painter's Studio.*
          Princeton Architectural Press, New York, 2009.

p. 25   'I conducted a small longitudinal study'
        Charlotte Wood. *Looking for Trouble: Problem-finding*
          processes in literary creativity. PhD thesis, University of
          New South Wales, School of the Arts & Media, Faculty
          of Arts & Social Sciences, 2016.

p. 29   'this joining of unlike things'
        'The *Rumpus* interview with Richard Ford'. Interview by Ben
          Pfeiffer. *The Rumpus.* 26 November 2014.

p. 29   'It's nearly always unintentional'
        'Margaret Drabble: The art of fiction no. 70'. Interview by
        Barbara Milton. *Paris Review*, issue 74, 1978.

p. 30   'shallow and false and unsatisfactory'
        Peter Carey. Interview by Kate Grenville and Sue Woolfe.
        Making Stories: How ten Australian novels were written.
        Allen & Unwin, Sydney, 1993 (2001).

p. 37   'I do not so much write a book as sit up with it'
        Annie Dillard. *The Writing Life*. Harper Perennial, New York,
        1990.

p. 38   'It was time out'
        Joan London. Interview by Charlotte Wood. *The Writer's
        Room*. Allen & Unwin, Sydney, 2016.

p. 38   'I just hang over the typewriter'
        'William Maxwell: The art of fiction no. 71'. Interview by
        John Seabrook. *Paris Review*, issue 85, 1982.

p. 40   'anguish and rapture'
        Katherine Mansfield. Letter to Hugh Walpole, 27 October
        1920. *Katherine Mansfield: Letters and journals*. Selected
        and edited by C.K. Stead. Allen Lane, London, 1977.

p. 42   'Beauty is truth, truth beauty'
        John Keats, 'Ode on a Grecian Urn' (first published
        anonymously in *Annals of the Fine Arts for 1819*). *Ode on
        a Grecian Urn, the Eve of St. Agnes: And Other Poems with
        Biographical Sketch, Introduction and Notes*. Houghton
        Mifflin Co, Boston, 1915.

p. 43   'paying attention is a moral act'
        Iris Murdoch. *The Sovereignty of Good*. Routledge, London,
        1970.
        Note: This is not a verbatim quotation. Murdoch
        acknowledges borrowing this contextual use of 'attention'
        from Simone Weil, possibly from *Gravity and Grace*.
        Routledge & Kegan Paul, London, 1952.

4. UNCONSCIOUS BIAS

p. 49   'sleep in the same room as it'
        'Joan Didion: The art of fiction no. 71'. Interview by Linda
        Kuehl. *Paris Review*, issue 74, 1978.

p. 49   'the wanting system'
        Mark Solms, Professor of Neuropsychology at the University
        of Cape Town. Interview by Melvyn Bragg. *In Our Time*,
        BBC 4, 4 March 2004.

p. 50   'I do a lot of work in dreams'
        'Rodney Hall at the Bendigo Writers Festival'. Interview by
        Sarah L'Estrange. *The Book Show*, ABC Radio National,
        19 December 2018.

p. 53   'At times she felt on the edge of discovering'
        Charlotte Wood. *The Weekend*. Allen & Unwin, Sydney, 2019.

p. 53   'To be a fool'
        'Anne Sexton, The Art of Poetry no. 15'. Interview by Barbara
        Kevles. *Paris Review*, issue 52, 1971.

5. TAKE AN OBJECT

p. 55   'the radio documentary that lit the fuse'
         'Exposed to moral danger'. *Hindsight*, ABC Radio National,
         19 July 2009.

p. 58   'take an object'
         Barbara Rose. 'Jasper Johns: "Take an object. Do something
         to it. Do something else to it."' *Royal Academy Magazine*,
         7 September 2017.

p. 58   'I refer to such intangibles as colors'
         Uta Hagen. *Respect for Acting*. Macmillan, New York, 1973.

p. 59   'There is the literal surface of life'
         Amanda Lohrey. Interview by Charlotte Wood. *The Writer's
         Room*. Allen & Unwin, Sydney, 2016.

6. STRANGE BEDFELLOWS

p. 66   'In the soft dewy morning'
         Charlotte Wood. *The Natural Way of Things*. Allen & Unwin,
         Sydney, 2015.

7. LETTING IN THE LIGHT

p. 79   'even while she looked at the mass, the line, the colour'
         Virginia Woolf. *To the Lighthouse*. Hogarth Press, London,
         1927.

p. 86   'It pushes me away from the painting'
         'Painter Jude Rae on the still life and the artist's path'.
         Interview by Charlotte Wood. *The Writer's Room*
         podcast, episode 8, 21 January 2021.

p. 91   'What is the use of saying one is indifferent'
Virginia Woolf. Diary entry, 11 May 1927. *A Writer's Diary*.
Hogarth Press, London, 1953.

8. CAT AND BABY

p. 101   'Know your own bone'
Annie Dillard. *The Writing Life*. Harper Perennial, New York,
1990.

p. 101   'When your Daemon is in charge'
Joan London. Interview by Charlotte Wood. *The Writer's
Room*. Allen & Unwin, Sydney, 2016.

9. AN ELEMENT OF LIGHTNESS

p. 109   'an element of lightness and playfulness'
Sigrid Nunez. Interview by Charlotte Wood. *American Writers
Museum*. YouTube, 24 September 2020.

p. 110   'I tend to shift tone from paragraph to paragraph'
Anne Enright. In conversation with Professor Gerardine
Meaney. University College Dublin School of English,
Drama and Film. YouTube, 26 October 2017.

p. 111   'Satire is dependent on strong beliefs'
Anita Brookner. *The Spectator*, 23 March 1989.

p. 111   'I'm incredibly idealistic'
Wayne Macauley. Interview by Charlotte Wood. *The Writer's
Room*. Allen & Unwin, Sydney, 2016.

p. 112   'I knew what I was doing'
Kim Scott. Interview by Charlotte Wood. *The Writer's Room*.
Allen & Unwin, Sydney, 2016.

p. 112   'Beauty, Power, Humour and Land'
Melissa Lucashenko. 'Writing as a sovereign act'. *Meanjin*,
Summer 2018.

p. 115   'That was [a] moment of excitement'
'George Saunders: The WD interview'. Interview by Tyler
Moss. *Writer's Digest*, 9 May 2018.

p. 116   'unflinching dissections of middle class domestic life'
Margalit Fox. 'Alice Thomas Ellis dies at 72; writer about
spiritual and mundane'. *New York Times*, 12 March 2005.

p. 116   'determined to be pleasant'
Alice Thomas Ellis. *Unexplained Laughter*. Little, Brown,
London, 2012.

p. 118   'this really uptight White woman from New England'
'Elizabeth Strout: "Nobody was even remotely interested in
my writing"'. Interview by Alice Jones. iNews. co.uk,
5 June 2018.

10. THE PAINT ITSELF

p. 122   'The complex struggle between order and chaos'
Laurie Fendrich. 'Why abstract painting still matters'.
Chronicle of Higher Education, 30 April 1999.

p. 122   '[The] paint itself'
Laurie Fendrich. 'Painting 2.0'. 'Brainstorm' (blog), *Chronicle
of Higher Education*, 8 July 2008.

p. 123   'it is that something itself'

        Samuel Beckett. 'Dante . . . Bruno. Vico . . . Joyce'. *Our Exagmination Round His Factification for Incamination of Work in Progress: James Joyce/Finnegans Wake.* Shakespeare & Co., Paris, 1929.

        Lloyd Jones. Interview by Charlotte Wood. *The Writer's Room.* Allen & Unwin, Sydney, 2016.

p. 123   'Gornick's voice . . . does not just tell the story'

        Michelle Orange. 'Vivian Gornick's voice'. *New Yorker*, 29 May 2015.

p. 128   'And after all the weather was ideal.'

        Katherine Mansfield. 'The Garden Party'. *Selected Stories.* Text Publishing, Melbourne, 2012.

p. 128   '124 was spiteful. Full of a baby's venom.'

        Toni Morrison. *Beloved.* Random House, London, 2008.

p. 130   'He's a *painter*'

        'A picture of the painter Howard Hodgkin'. *Imagine.* Presented by Alan Yentob. BBC One, Spring 2006.

p. 130   'but I want very, very much to do the thing that Valery said'

        Ernst van Alphen. *Francis Bacon and the Loss of Self.* Harvard University Press, Cambridge, Mass., 1993.

11. READING ISN'T SHOPPING

p. 140   'To seek to see oneself in a work of art'

        Rebecca Mead. 'The scourge of "relatability"'. *New Yorker*, 1 August 2014.

p. 142 'Do you like Olive Kitteridge as a person?'
Elizabeth Strout. *Olive Kitteridge*. Random House, New York, 2008.

p. 144 'I think they find Ari difficult'
Tegan Bennett Daylight '"The difficulty is the point":
Teaching spoon-fed students how to really read'.
The Guardian, 24 December 2017.

p. 148 'epiphany peddling and empathy porn'
Aleksandar Hemon. 'Six writers on the genius of Marcel
Proust'. *Literary Hub*, 11 July 2016.

p. 148 'A book is a little empathy machine'
Toby Litt. 'Neil Gaiman: Libraries are cultural "seed corn"'.
The Guardian, 18 November 2014.

p. 148 'the most important set of understandings'
'President Barack Obama & Marilynne Robinson:
A conversation—II'. *New York Review*, 19 November
2015.

p. 149 'Empathy depends on perceived likeness'
Sarah Sentilles. *Draw Your Weapons*. Text Publishing,
Melbourne, 2017.

12. THE OUTSIDE VOICE

p. 153 'no matter how much we claim to embrace creativity'
Jessica Olien. 'Inside the box: People don't actually like
creativity'. *Slate*, 6 December 2013.

p. 154 'rejection is *good for creativity*'
    'Don't get mad, get creative: Social rejection can fuel
    imaginative thinking, study shows'. *ScienceDaily*,
    21 August 2012.

p. 155 'look at that dirty thing'
    Australian Biography: Rosalie Gascoigne. Interview by Robin
    Hughes. Film Australia Collection, National Film and
    Sound Archive, 1999. Excerpts broadcast on YouTube,
    March 2007.

p. 155 'We are talking about expression'
    Nick Miller. 'Sylvie Guillem: Life in progress—the greatest
    dancer of our time calls it quits'. *Sydney Morning Herald*,
    14 August 2015.

p. 156 'Deeper in my mind'
    Alexis Wright. 'The big book about small town Australia that
    travelled the world'. *The Guardian*, 8 September 2017.

p. 157 'that rare phenomenon: a natural painter'
    John McDonald. 'Lucy Culliton's Eye of the Beholder survey
    of her work urges recollection of the long familiar'. *Sydney
    Morning Herald*, 24 October 2014.

p. 157 'I was an artist!'
    Charlotte Wood. 'Painter Ann Thomson: Driven to
    abstraction'. *The Saturday Paper*, 12–18 December 2015.

13. AFRAID OF THE DARK

p. 163 'felt the kind of electrical twang'
    Elizabeth Strout. *Anything is Possible*. Random House, New
    York, 2017.

p. 163 'But I will tell you this'
'Elizabeth Strout: *Olive Kitteridge*'. Interview by Harriett
Gilbert. *World Book Club*. BBC World Service,
6 September 2020.

p. 164 'the shield of feminine passivity'
Helen Garner. 'The insults of age'. *The Monthly*, May 2015.

p. 168 'it taught women to devour themselves'
'Winning women: Eimear McBride and Charlotte Wood
(Melbourne Writers Festival 2016)'. Schwartz Media.
YouTube, 8 December 2016.

p. 168 'hot material'
'Jonathan Franzen: The art of fiction no. 207'. Interview by
Stephen J. Burn. *Paris Review*, issue 195, 2010.

p. 169 'You can choose what you write'
'George Saunders: "The things we felt about American culture
couldn't be reached by simple realism. It had to be a
little nutty"'. Interview by Alex Clark. *The Guardian*,
13 March 2014.

p. 170 'You mean mildly peeved, or really raging?'
'Feminist dystopia'. Margaret Atwood interview by Ann
Friedman. *Call Your Girlfriend* podcast, 10 November 2017.

14. ON GODS AND GHOSTS

p. 176 'Some experiences in life are so fundamental'
Norman Mailer. *The Spooky Art: Thoughts on writing*.
Random House, New York, 2003.

p. 186   'it awakens you spiritually'
        Janine Burke. Interview by Charlotte Wood. *The Writer's Room*, issue 5, October 2015.

15. *BETWEEN A WOLF AND A DOG*

p. 188   '*Dear Chris,*' he writes.
        Georgia Blain. *Between a Wolf and a Dog*. Scribe, Melbourne, 2016.

16. USEFUL, PLEASURABLE, STRANGE

p. 201   'The biological, cognitive and emotional changes'
        Margit Cox Henderson. 'The paradox of aging: the happiness U-curve'. margithenderson.com, 4 March 2018.

p. 202   'Arthur Krystal sneers at the recent proliferation'
        Arthur Krystal. 'Why we can't tell the truth about aging'. *New Yorker*, 28 October 2019.

p. 203   'Old People Behaving Hilariously'
        Neil Genzlinger. 'Review: "The 100-Year-Old Man Who Climbed Out the Window and Disappeared"'. *New York Times*, 7 May 2015.

p. 204   'one of the good ones'
        Richard Roe. 'Counting down the days in God's waiting room'. *Good Weekend*, 17 November 2018.

p. 204   'in an affluent Melbourne suburb'
        Peter Thomson. Letter to the editor. *Good Weekend*, 1 December 2018.

p. 206 'a transformation in beauty as much as in biology'
James Hillman. *The Force of Character: And the lasting life.*
Ballantine, New York, 1999.

p. 206 'Don't think good or bad'
Jerry Saltz. *How to Be an Artist.* Riverhead, New York, 2020.

p. 206 'I am large, I contain multitudes.'
Walt Whitman. *Leaves of Grass.* HarperCollins, London,
2015.

p. 206 'I'd rather risk an ugly surprise'
'An interview with Helen Frankenthaler'. *Artforum,*
October 1965.

p. 207 'Take an object'
Barbara Rose. 'Jasper Johns: "Take an object. Do something
to it. Do something else to it."' *Royal Academy Magazine,*
7 September 2017.

p. 207 'robbed of the richness of who we are'
Blake Morrison and Susie Orbach. 'The talking cure'.
The Guardian, 9 February 2005.

17. THE RAPTURE

p. 216 'when persons with prepared minds'
Mihaly Csikszentmihalyi. *Creativity: The psychology of
discovery and invention.* Harper Perennial, New York,
2013.

p. 219 'She had lost, she felt, a great deal'
Charlotte Wood. *The Weekend.* Allen & Unwin, Sydney, 2019.

ACKNOWLEDGEMENTS

Thank you to friends and colleagues whose example and conversation have enriched this book, especially Lucy Culliton, Tegan Bennett Daylight, Peter Godwin, Vicki Hastrich, Lucinda Holdforth, Malcolm Knox, Alison Manning, Heather Mitchell, Ailsa Piper, David Raubenheimer, Hannie Rayson, Anne-Louise Sarks, Sarah Sentilles, Peter Simpson, Steve Simpson, Sue Smith, Carolyn Swindell, Ann Thomson. Thanks to those who generously allowed me to quote from their work or interviews, especially Karla Dickens, Tegan Bennett Daylight, Melissa Lucashenko, Jude Rae, Kim Scott, Alexis Wright. Thank you to the editors who first commissioned pieces that became some of these chapters, especially Lucy Clark and Ashley Hay. For their essential guidance and friendship over so many years, deepest thanks to Jenny Darling, Jane Palfreyman and Ali Lavau.

Thank you to everyone at Allen & Unwin for their professionalism and kindness. Deepest gratitude to my family and Sean McElvogue for their enduring support and love.

Last, my thanks to every artist whose name appears in this book; your spirit keeps me going.